Praise for Steve W...   eBay 101

"I wish I'd had this book when I started on eBay. It's a virtual encyclopedia of tips for selling successfully on eBay–information that takes years to learn."

— *Jane Corn, eBay Top Reviewer*

"A street-smart guide to selling on eBay!"

— *Ina Steiner, Editor, AuctionBytes.com*

"Ideal for the beginner and useful for the experienced eBayer, too— a gold mine of valuable and up-to-date information!"

— *John Landahl, author of "Estate Sale Prospecting for Fun and Profit with Craigslist and eBay"*

"What I really like about *eBay 101* is that Steve has actually done this stuff. Too many people claim to be "experts" who haven't really sold that much. *eBay 101* comes from someone with real-life experience making money on eBay."

— *Skip McGrath, eBay Gold PowerSeller and author of "Titanium eBay"*

"Anyone who is interested in online retailing should do themselves a favor: get a copy of *eBay 101* and read it cover to cover."

— *Jeff Lippincott, Top Reviewer, Amazon.com*

Also by Steve Weber

The Home-Based Bookstore: Start Your Own Business Selling Used Books on Amazon, eBay or Your Own Web Site

Sell on Amazon: A Guide to Amazon's Marketplace, Seller Central, and Fulfillment by Amazon programs

eBay 101

Selling on eBay

For part-time or
full-time income

Beginner to PowerSeller in 90 days

By Steve Weber

All Rights Reserved © 2011 by Stephen W. Weber

Published by Stephen W. Weber

Printed in the United States of America

Weber Books   www.WeberBooks.com

Author: Steve Weber

Editor: Julie Bird

13-digit ISBN: 978-0-9772406-3-0

10-digit ISBN: 0-9772406-3-0

Contents

Warning and Disclaimer

Introduction

Starting a business on eBay is perhaps your fastest route to the American Dream. The payoff can be high, and the barriers to entry are low. The world's most popular online marketplace, eBay has millions of registered buyers waiting to do business with you. For less than $100 and very little risk, you can start an eBay venture with profit margins rivaling those of any business. Exactly how much money you earn depends mostly on how much effort you put into your new enterprise and how efficiently you operate it.

eBay provides a fair, level playing field for beginners and seasoned pros alike. If you're already employed, you can begin your eBay business as a part-time venture, as I did. If your eBay profits grow bigger than your paycheck, you can quit your day job and enjoy one of the most rewarding experiences of your life: building a thriving business from scratch.

Nothing is more empowering than building your own business to support yourself and your family. You don't need a store or a warehouse or delivery trucks to sell on eBay. You don't need an MBA or inside connections with wholesalers or drop-shippers. The only requirements are a willingness to learn and a commitment to running an honest business.

No business is better suited to the one-person company than eBay. You can start small—perhaps with some of your own unwanted possessions—and you can invest your profits in new inventory and expand at your own pace. If you'd like to earn just a few hundred dollars a month to supplement your current income, you can keep the enterprise part time. If you want to take four months off during the summer, you can. If you decide to go full time, it's certainly possible to earn more than $40,000 a year working on your own. Whether you begin as a home-based business or a sideline to an existing business, the opportunities are vast. Today is a good time to start.

I began my online selling career in 2001 by selling some of my old books on Half.com, now owned by eBay. I listed a couple dozen of my unwanted tomes and was amazed to see how quickly they sold. I couldn't wait to find new books to list. Impulsively, I withdrew $80 from my meager savings to buy four bags of used paperbacks from a local shop. Several of the books turned out to be worthless, but one book sold immediately for $23, and within a few days, after selling just half of those books, I had doubled my $80 investment. I was hooked.

I immediately hauled a carload of books home from a library sale and worked straight through the weekend listing them for sale. I quit my job two months later and never looked back. In the meantime, I've expanded my business to eBay and other sites, racking up $1.4 million in sales to 130,000 customers in all 50 states and 31 foreign countries. With the profits, I've paid off my debts and moved from a cramped apartment to a nice house. I did it all myself, with no bosses and no employees. And it all started with that $80 I spent on that first batch of books and the impulse to see what was possible. Meanwhile, lots of people have been even more successful on eBay than I have.

All this would have been impossible just 10 or 15 years ago. To be a retailer before eBay, you had to first assemble a wide range of mer-chandise—enough variety to lure people in your door. You needed to lease retail space. You needed employees. You had to pay through the nose to advertise, and then you would pray some customers showed up with money in hand. If something went sufficiently wrong, you lost your shirt.

Today, you can market instantly to a worldwide pool of millions of ready buyers—even as a beginning seller—and you don't need to advertise.

I can't guarantee you'll make money selling stuff on eBay. Most sellers don't get rich, and some even go broke. This is not a get-rich-quick scheme. It's hard work. But it's a lot more satisfying to work hard at your own business than for someone else—you reap the rewards. And your odds of success will be much better by following the hard-earned advice in this book.

When I started, I knew nothing about online selling, but it's amazing how fast you can learn by doing something you enjoy. A few people tried to talk me out of writing what you hold in your hands right now, saying I should keep what I've learned to myself. "Don't help your competition," they warned. But I don't look at it that way. Since you're reading this book, you're either interested in selling on eBay or have already started. The ideas in this book will help make your business successful faster than trial and error. And if you run a good operation, that helps me; if you make your eBay customers happy, maybe they'll buy from me next time. And those buyers will tell their friends about shopping at eBay, and so on.

My theory about selling online is that everyone can win. The more people who become buyers and sellers in this worldwide network, the more valuable it is for everyone to belong. It's a virtuous cycle. Buyers can find more of what they want, and sellers have more buyers every day.

How eBay works

eBay is an Internet-based auction and shopping venue where people and businesses around the world buy and sell goods and services. Millions of items—baby clothes, toasters, pool tables, rare stamps, automobiles, and other paraphernalia—are listed and sold every day.

eBay also operates an online payment company, PayPal, which makes electronic payments fast, easy and safe. Buyers and sellers rate each other with "feedback," allowing traders to check each other's reputation before transacting.

And so for the budding entrepreneur, eBay provides the essential ingredients for a thriving business: a steady stream of customers and a safe trading environment.

Before you begin

Even if you feel ready to start selling on eBay, take a few weeks to get familiar with the marketplace:

- **Buy something from 10 different sellers.** If you haven't yet participated on eBay, this will get your feet wet. You'll start building your feedback record. And nothing teaches you the ropes faster than seeing a variety of eBay transactions from the buyer's side.

Those 10 transactions will all be unique because each seller is different. Take notes on how each seller handles his or her business. Study their listing descriptions, their responsiveness, and their shipping practices. Ask yourself: Why did you buy from them instead of another seller? With each transaction, you'll likely see room for improvement. Figure out how you can correct what those sellers are doing wrong and improve on what they're doing right.

Make no mistake, you're about to enter a great competition. To achieve at a high level, you must offer good merchandise and great service. Your first step is studying your competitors. Don't worry, there's still plenty of room for more eBay sellers. You'll find there's an infinite number of ways to succeed.

Getting active on eBay might also dispel some preconceived notions holding you back. eBay isn't just an online yard sale, and it's not just for collectors or penny-pinchers. Virtually any kind of legal product or service can be marketed, so there's a built-in market for practically everything—new, used and collectible items of every kind.

Becoming an active buyer on eBay also gives you a keen insight into precisely how shoppers *find* the stuff they buy on eBay. Armed with that knowledge, you'll be a superior seller. For a thorough tutorial on searching and browsing eBay, see this page:

http://pages.ebay.com/help/find/find_ov.html

- **Don't go hogwild.** Naturally, you want to get your new business off the ground as quickly as possible. But take a deep breath. Don't blow $5,000 on a truckload of merchandise unless you know what you're doing. If something looks like the "chance of a lifetime," sleep on it. Read this book all the way through. Then read it again. To thrive over the long term, you need to develop a set of business practices—everything from inventory gathering to selling, shipping, and handling questions from buyers—that you can repeat time after time as efficiently as possible. Rome wasn't built in a day, and neither is any successful eBay business.

Get more help

Every once in a while, you might have a question or a technical problem. Fortunately, help is just a few clicks away with eBay's "Live Help" feature.

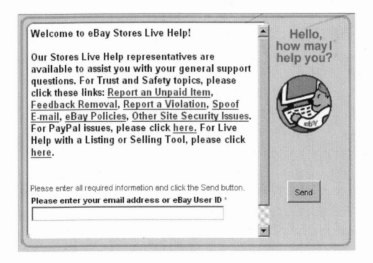

Click **Help** at the top of any eBay page, then **Contact Us.** You can contact an eBay representative by clicking **Live Help**, which launches a chat window where you can ask your question. Representatives are on duty 24 hours a day, seven days a week.

You can also use e-mail to contact customer support by clicking the **Contact Us** link that appears on most help pages, or visit this page: **http://pages.ebay.com/help/contact_us/_base/ index_selection.html**

You may find the glossary and index in the back of this book helpful. And for further sources of help and advice, see the section called "More Great eBay Resources."

Ready, set, sell!

To begin selling on eBay, you'll need to register at eBay.com unless you're already a member. Click the "Register" link at the top of the page. Becoming a seller is a free, one-time process where you verify your identity, confirm your e-mail address, and indicate how you'll pay your seller fees. You must offer a way for buyers to pay you with a credit card service such as PayPal, which is a separate registration process you can initiate at PayPal.com. You can also accept checks and other forms of payment approved for use on eBay.

To verify your identity, you'll need to provide a credit or debit card and in certain cases, you'll need to provide your checking account details. Your card won't actually be charged unless you use it to pay your eBay fees after you list and sell items.

If you don't have a credit card or don't want to put it on file with eBay, you can establish your identity with ID Verify, which costs $5.

Register your business

You can register at eBay as an individual or a business. It's the same process, but registering as a business lets you add your business name to your account. If you're already registered at eBay as an individual, you can change your account to a business account.

You should have a business account if you:

- Sell items you've purchased to resell.

- Sell items you've made yourself for resale.

- Sell a large volume of items regularly.

- Sell new items you haven't bought for your personal use.

- Sell as a trading assistant.

- Buy eBay items for use in a business.

There are several advantages to registering as a business on eBay. Your business name will be displayed in all communication received by buyers, such as e-mails and invoices. Also, business sellers can display contact information, return policies, and terms and conditions in their listings. Business sellers outside North America can provide the value-added tax percentage when using the "Sell Your Item" Web form.

To change your eBay registration from personal to business, click **My eBay** at the top of any page. Then:

- Click **Personal Information** under the **My Account** heading.

- Click **Edit** next to **Account Type.**

- Select **Business**, then click **Continue.**

- Type your business name, then click **Change to Business Account.**

In registering with eBay, you agree to abide by eBay's rules and regulations in its User Agreement, which stipulates, among other things:

- Your eBay sales and purchases are legally binding contracts.

- You agree to pay eBay fees resulting from your listings and sales.

- You won't sell prohibited items.

For more information, see the eBay User Agreement:

http://pages.ebay.com/help/policies/user-agreement.html

Sell your item

To list your first item for sale on eBay, click **Sell** to enter your title, description, price, payment method, shipping terms, and a photo. eBay's **Sell Your Item** form guides you through these steps:

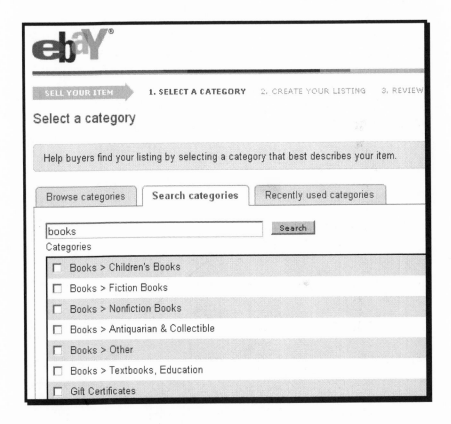

Build your listing

The **Sell Your Item** form guides you through the steps of creating a listing:

- **Select a category.**

- **Write a title and description.** Use facts and persuasion to interest buyers.

- **Enter Item Specifics.** This eBay feature helps shoppers find your merchandise.

- **Upload pictures.** You'll sell at higher prices with photos of your item.

- **Select a listing format.** Auction, fixed price, or store inventory.

- **Select a price.** Start auctions low to draw in bidders.

- **Select a listing duration.** Auctions can last just one day or up to 10 days.

- **Provide shipping and return information.**

- **Select listing upgrades.** Pay more to get more attention.

Each of these elements is explained in detail in subsequent sections of this book.

Nail down details

In listing your item for sale, your main task is to inform buyers exactly what is for sale, present your merchandise in the most favorable light, and generate competition among buyers. Pay particular attention to these elements of your listing:

- **Item Title.** Your title is the single most important element of your auction, so give it careful thought. You can have the most dazzling photo, eloquent description, and other doodads, but none of it will matter without a compelling title that makes buyers click to find out more.

Your title can use up to 55 characters, so use as many as possible to maximum effect. Sixty-five percent of eBay buyers find their item by searching with keywords such as "Kodak digital camera." Each character you use is precious, so follow these tips:

- Include general keywords such as "DVD player."

- Include descriptive words. For example, the title for your DVD player auction could include the brand name and DVD formats it supports.

- Avoid unusual abbreviations.

- Look for popular words likely to be searched by shoppers for that item.

- Include important attributes and promises such as "New" or "Free Shipping."

- Use verbs when possible such as **save** and **buy.**

Item description. Use descriptive, short sentences. Where appropriate, use bold text and bulleted lists to make the text easy to scan. Be sure to include these basic elements:

- **Type.** Model number or style. (Dell 1660 Laser Printer).

- **Brand.** Manufacturer or label. (Wrangler jeans).

- **Condition.** New, used, reconditioned, vintage, etc.

- **Value.** Original manufacturer's suggested retail price, estimated or appraised value (Originally retailed for $50).

- **Technical details.** Size, measurements, technical specifications (100-watt speaker). Year of model.

- **Spell check your listing.** Before submitting your listing, use the spell-check feature in the Description section of the Sell Your Item form. Misspelled words will be highlighted, along with a list of suggested corrections. After the spell check, you can save or cancel your changes, then continue with the Sell Your Item form.

Plan your auction

eBay sellers have a multitude of selling options illustrated in the following table.

	How It Works	Length
Auction	Sell to the **highest bidder**. You may also include a **Buy It Now** price. **Quantity:** One or multiple items. **Where:** Your listing appears in the eBay category (or categories) you choose and in search results.	1, 3, 5, 7, or 10 days. Real estate auctions may run for 30 days. **Note:** 1-day listings are not available for eBay Motor Vehicles categories in the U.S. or Canada.
Fixed Price	Buyers can purchase immediately without bidding. **Quantity:** Offer one or multiple items. **Where:** In the eBay category (or categories) you choose and in search results.	3, 5, 7, or 10 days. Real estate auctions may run for 30 days.
Best Offer	You can designate listings to consider "Best Offers" from buyers (for example, "$50 or Best Offer"). Buyers who make an offer might be able to purchase at their price.	Fixed Price or Buy It Now
Store	List at set price, no bidding. Longer duration but limited visibility. **Quantity:** Offer one or multiple items for one Buy It Now price. **Where:** Your store, store searches, regular eBay search and browse results if there are 30 or fewer Online Auction and Fixed Price listings	30 days Good 'Til Cancelled - Renews automatically every 30 days until the item sells or you end the listing. Insertion fees charged every 30-day period.
Classified Ad	Enables sellers to make contact with many interested buyers, not just the highest bidder. There's no obligation for buyers who contact a seller. **Where:** Ad appears in the eBay category of your choice, for supported categories.	Varies by category. Options include 30 days and Good 'Til Cancelled. Real Estate has various listing durations.

Make a picture worth $1,000

Buyers are much more likely to bid and buy when they can see a photograph of the item. Since your customer can't physically pick up and inspect your merchandise, you've got to make up for it with illustration. Would you spend much money on something if you didn't know what it looked like? Probably not. (There are a few exceptions—if you're selling an inexpensive book or video, you can probably get by with using eBay's "stock" photo of the cover artwork—but even then, you're at a disadvantage with other sellers if you don't back it up with a good description.)

If you don't display a picture of your item, buyers may wonder whether you really have the item in stock, or are hiding some horrible defect. If you don't already use a digital camera, now is the time to get one and learn to use it. An inexpensive used camera with two megapixels will work just fine for eBay pictures. You should be able to find a suitable camera on eBay for $25 or less.

- **eBay Picture Manager.** eBay allows you to add one picture to each of your listings for free. As many as 11 more photos can be added to a listing but extra fees apply. Picture Manager is a subscription service offered by eBay for $9.99 per month. Instead of uploading pictures one at a time, you can add multiple pictures to listings and easily change and remove pictures. For more information, see:

http://pages.ebay.com/picture_manager/

Get free image hosting. You can save a lot of money by opening an account with Photobucket.com and using its free service to display photos in your eBay descriptions. Here are instructions for linking your images to your eBay descriptions:

http://tutorials.photobucket.com/tutorial_50.html

There are several other popular image hosting sites:

http://www.myeasypics.com/
http://www.auctiva.com/

To make your pictures effective, keep it simple. Focus in closely on the item to eliminate distracting backgrounds. Using a piece of poster board or cloth as a backdrop can improve your image. Use natural lighting when possible to reduce the shadows that result from a flash, or augment your natural lighting with one or two lamps. A couple of student desktop study lamps can produce adequate lighting.

Take great eBay photos

By Camera Jim

- **Use natural light.** If you had to choose just one light to use for product photography, it should be the light coming from a bright window without direct sunlight. That's because this light is both large (which is what makes it diffuse and soft) and it is directional, which can help show off the shape and texture of your subject.

- **Use a tripod for sharp photos.** A solid support for your camera is another important tool because it prevents blurring due to camera motion. Most "out of focus" shots aren't really unfocused, they're blurry because the camera moved slightly during exposure.

- **Create a second light with a reflector.** Add light to lighten or fill shadows on the other side of the subject. Your fill light can be simply a flat piece of poster board, propped up and used as a reflector. This controls the highlight and shadow values in your scene. If the main light is too strong in relation to the fill light, the highlights will be washed out and the shadows will be too dark. If the fill light is too strong, you might wipe out the shadows completely and lose the sense of shape they give your subject. Fortunately, digital cameras allow an immediate re-view of your results, so you can easily experiment with your fill light.

- **Use basic artificial light.** If you don't have a handy window or you need to shoot at night, you can use plain old tungsten (incandescent) lights. These are regular household bulbs, the kind you use in table lamps. Two 150-watt bulbs are enough, as long as you remember to use that tripod. You can use these bulbs in photographic reflectors with light stands (available on eBay or from a camera shop) or simple clamp-on reflectors of the sort sold at home centers for $10 or less. For best results, preset your camera's "white balance" control to "tungsten" or "incandescent."

- **Diffuse lights for window-like softness.** You can turn those artificial lights into soft, window-like sources by aiming them through translucent white material (a sheet of tracing paper, a piece of white plastic, etc.) or by bouncing them off reflectors.

- **Use a light tent.** This lighting tool is used often by professional product photographers, and commercially made light tents have become popu-lar with eBay sellers. Search on eBay for "light tent" and you'll find hundreds for sale in the **Cameras and Photos** category. These are small, white, cube-shaped tents with one open side where you insert your camera lens.

- **The milk jug light tent.** The simplest and cheapest form of a light tent for small objects is a plastic milk jug with the bottom cut off. The white plastic diffuses the light inside the jug. Shoot through the neck or a hole cut in the side.

Camera Jim is a longtime eBay seller of photography supplies at http://stores.ebay.com/CameraJim. For more information on how to enhance your auctions with photos, see Jim's free tutorials at http://www.camerajim.com.

Get specific

During the listing process in some eBay categories, you have the opportunity to give more details about your item, such as its color, size, style, or other information. For example, in the "camera" category, you could specify the brand, lens size, resolution, and condition (new, used or refurbished.) In the illustration below, you can see the column of **Item Specifics** in the left column of this eBay camera category, which helps buyers narrow in on exactly what they're looking for. The feature helps buyers find your item, since they can search or sort listings based on these criteria.

Item specifics also appear within your listing, augmenting your item description. You should use the Item Specifics feature whenever it's available during the listing process, since it's free, creates more exposure for your item and draws more bidders, helping you sell at higher prices.

● **Use Pre-filled Item Information.** It's faster to list standardized media items like books, videos, music and video games by typing in their product codes, known as ISBNs or UPCs. These numerals usually appear above the barcode on the back of the product.

Listings created this way are automatically populated with eBay's stock images and specifications. This pre-filled item information saves listing time and makes your listing look professional. To find pre-filled information, click **Find your product** under the Pre-filled item information section on the Sell Your Item form.

● **Find your listing.** You can review your listings in My eBay or by searching for the Item Number you receive at the end of the listing process. You'll also receive an e-mail confirming your listing with a link to your item page. It may take buyers a while to find your item—listings don't show up on eBay's pages immediately, and sometimes don't appear in search results for several hours.

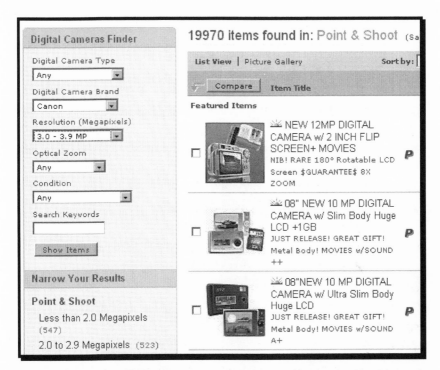

- **Revise your listing.** If you've made a mistake or change your mind about your listing, it's sometimes possible to change the title, description, price or shipping terms. Which elements you can change depend on how much time is left on the listing an d whether it has received any bids. From My eBay, click on **Selling** and scroll through your list of items. On the item you want to change, click the pull-down menu in the **Action** column and click **Revise.** You can make changes on the Revise Your Item page. Sections in gray can no longer be changed.

Write a top-notch item description

By: thedugout

- **Stick to the facts, not fluff.** Don't act like a used car salesman. Write a thorough, factual description of your item and its condition. This gives buyers the confidence to bid.

- **Put yourself in the buyer's place.** Anticipate the questions they'll have, and answer them in your description. Is your item new or used? Are there scratches or other defects?

- **Don't over-promise.** Listing at least one flaw, even a minor one, bolsters the confidence of bidders. It makes a statement: "I'm not hiding anything."

- **If in doubt, don't leave it out.** Unless your item is brand new, you've got to explain the condition. Even if a flaw is barely noticeable, it's best to mention it in your description. Including a close-up photograph of the flaw is a good idea, too. Collectors are especially interested in the condition of the items they buy, since it affects the value.

- **Maintain a professional tone.** State your terms of sale firmly, but in a positive light. Give bidders reasons they *should* bid, not why they *shouldn't* bid. If you list a series of negative or demanding statements in your auction, buyers will click right on to the next seller.

Thedugout is a longtime eBay seller of sports memorabilia and many other items. See: http://myworld.ebay.com/thedugout

Sell like a pro

The key to the salability of any item is its condition. For collectibles especially, as much as 90 percent of the value depends on the condition. So in most cases it's best to pass up merchandise with major, ugly flaws.

Buyers understand that used items will show some wear, but nobody wants an item that looks abused. No matter how many precautions you take to warn a customer about an item's defects, you run the risk of ending up with an unhappy buyer who didn't read the description or forgot the details.

Sometimes condition problems will escape your attention and the customer will receive an item with a seemingly obvious flaw that you didn't explain in your eBay listing. Don't be shocked if the customer accuses you of fraud. Lots of eBay buyers assume you were the original user of the item and were intimately familiar with it. And so, the reasoning goes, if you failed to mention the condition problem, you're obviously untrustworthy.

If this happens, or I should say, *when* this happens, calmly explain that you weren't aware of the flaw. Offer a partial refund if the buyer is interested in keeping the item, or a full refund upon the return of the item, including shipping costs.

When you list a new item for sale, take the opportunity to give it a thorough inspection and spruce up its appearance. Sometimes a few moments spent polishing up an item brings in a higher selling price and results in a happier buyer. If possible, clean the surface with a spray detergent such as Fantastik. Stubborn dirt, ink, stains, and price tags can be removed with a solvent like Goo-Gone or Goof Off.

Grading the condition of used items. Here's a collection of terms used by sellers of miscellaneous new, used and collectible merchandise:

- **Mint.** This is as good as it gets. The item is new or good as brand new. If the item has ever been out of the box or handled, there's no evidence of the handling.

- **Near mint.** Practically as good as new, but it's evident the item has been out of the box or handled. Perhaps it's a stamp or a coin that has never been used, but has been handled.

- **Fine.** This is perhaps the lowest condition grading appropriate for a good collectible. Often you'll see a description like "Mint item in fine box."

- **Good.** This is below the collectible category, and is appropriate grade, for example, for a decorative vase with a small crack. This is a subjective grading, but mainly used to describe an item that is serviceable but has one or more obvious flaws.

- **Fair** or **Poor.** It's not very often that an item in fair or poor condition can be expected to draw bidders on eBay. Usually the item must have been very valuable when in original condition. For example, a piece of sculpture or other artwork by a famous artist that has significant damage might still fetch a nice price if it can be repaired or restored.

Price your item

Search eBay for listings of similar and identical listings to see the prices of your competitors. To see what the item has sold for previously, you can search eBay listings of auctions and listings that have already ended:

At the top of any page, click **Advanced Search.**

Enter keywords for your listing and, if appropriate, select a category. Check the checkbox for **Completed listings only.**

This shows the prices buyers have paid in the past, so it's a good guide to how much your item is likely to sell for. However, you might fare better or worse, depending on the details of previous transactions. On those completed transactions, check seller feedback, condition issues, and the competency of the descriptions.

Where should you set your price? If you want to sell your item at the highest price possible, it's essential to create competition among buyers. Many sellers believe that buyers respond best to auctions with low starting prices and no "reserve" price.

Having a low starting price makes it easier for you to attract the first bid. Once your auction has an initial bid, more bidders are likely to jump in. The more bids you have, the higher the final price is likely to be, simply because more bidders are watching your auction and ratcheting up the price. Many eBay buyers scan for items with lots of bids simply because they believe it's a sign of a bargain.

Following this strategy, many sellers start their auction at a price far below the true value of the item. Some sellers even start all their items at 1 cent. This can result in a bidding frenzy, drawing more attention to your auction.

Reserve Pricing. Your starting price isn't necessarily the lowest price you're willing to sell at. You can also set a **Reserve Price**, which is a secret minimum price you'll accept. The buyer can't see the reserve price, only an indication of whether the reserve has been met. You're not obligated to sell if no bids exceed the reserve. This enables you to set a lower starting price to jump-start bidding while ensuring the item doesn't sell at an unacceptably low price.

However, a reserve price can discourage bidders. They may quit watching an item if they bid and discover they haven't met the reserve. They may abandon the auction and look for other auctions where they expect to have a better chance of winning. For this reason, many sellers of high-value items include the words "No Reserve" in their auction title. Then shoppers know they will win the item with the high bid.

Multiple Item (Dutch) Auctions. If you have a group of identical items, you can auction all of them at the same time using a Dutch auction. Bidders can bid on any quantity, from one item up to the total number for sale. Winning bids are based on the highest bid per item. For example, imagine you have 25 identical T-shirts you want to sell for at least $5 each. You'd enter a quantity of 25 for your listing and a starting price of $5. Bidders state their maximum price per unit and the quantity they want.

Winners are determined in order of bid price for an item. A bid for 10 units at $7 ranks above a bid for 9 units at $6 per unit. In case of two bids with the same price per item, the earlier bid gets priority. Winning bidders pay the same price per unit as the lowest winning bid. So if the lowest winning bid is $5, the buyer who bid for 10 units at $7 pays only $50.

The auction alternative: fixed prices

You can sell items at a fixed price by adding a Buy It Now price to your listing. Fixed prices are often preferred by sellers who are selling commonly available, inexpensive items. For example, if you're selling a copy of a current bestselling book, it might sell faster with a Buy It Now fixed price because the buyer won't have to wait for an auction to end.

Auctioning the book is unlikely to bring a high price because bestsellers are in plentiful supply, and the item's value is no secret.

You can use Buy It Now with the Fixed Price listing format, or you can add a Buy It Now option to an auction listing. A feedback score of at least 10 is required for fixed-price listings.

- **Immediate Payment Required.** If you add a Buy It Now price in a listing, you can require the buyer to pay immediately using PayPal. The first buyer to complete a payment wins the item. This eliminates the possibility that you will waste time urging a reluctant buyer to pay. If you use the immediate payment feature, PayPal is the only payment method accepted for the listing.

- **Best Offer listing option.** When listing an item at a fixed price, if you use the Best Offer listing option, you are able to negotiate with buyers who are interested in your item but don't want to pay the full Buy It Now fixed price.

Best Offers are most commonly used for high-value items, but you can use it on any listing by checking the appropriate box on the listing form. Best Offers are good for 48 hours and are binding, just like a bid.

After receiving a Best Offer, you have these options:

- **Decline.** If you wish, you can explain your decision to the buyer.

- **Make a counteroffer.** If a buyer fails to respond within a reasonable period, the counteroffer can expire.

- **Allow the offer to expire.** The offer can expire after 48 hours or at the end of the listing, whichever is first.

You can set your eBay preferences to automatically accept or decline Best Offers based on price limits set by you.

Upgrade your listings

The more you can differentiate your listings from the competition on eBay, the more sales you're likely to get. For additional fees beyond the basic Insertion Fee, eBay offers a multitude of ways to highlight your item.

Shelling out the money to list upgrades is a gamble. The more you expect your item to sell for, the more likely the listing upgrades will pay off. For example, if you were selling a run-of-the-mill copy of a "Harry Potter" book and expected it to fetch $7, you wouldn't want to spend much on listing upgrades. But if your copy of "Harry Potter" was signed by the author and worth perhaps $5,000, the upgrade fees would be more likely to attract more bidders and ensure a higher selling price.

Fees are subject to change without notice, and some of the fees are different for eBay Motors. Keep on the lookout for special promotions when eBay periodically offers discounts on upgrades:

- **Gallery.** When shoppers browse categories or scan search results, Gallery pictures are visible alongside the item title. Because these small photos attract more attention than plain-text auction titles, adding a Gallery picture increases your chances of making a sale. According to eBay, items with Gallery pictures sell at a price 14 percent higher than those without the picture. Many sellers won't even consider listing an auction without using the Gallery feature because it's so inexpensive and a photo is so important to many buyers. A Gallery image lets eBay browsers know there's a photograph of your items, so it almost always results in more looks and bids.

- **Gallery Plus.** This feature displays a larger picture of your item in search results. When buyers place their mouse over your listing in search results, a larger image of your item is shown in a pop-up window.

- **Value Pack.** With this option, you choose a set of basic listing upgrades. It combines a Gallery picture, item subtitle, and listing designer at a discounted price.

- **Gallery Featured.** This promotional option causes your item to appear in the **Featured** section above the general Picture Gallery. The position of your listing depends on the time of your listing and the number of other Gallery Featured items currently in the category. When new, your listing will appear at the top of the page, but as more listings are added, your listing will be bumped down.

• **Highlight.** This option adds a colored band to your listing, adding emphasis compared with the white background on most other listings.

• **Border.** This surrounds your listing with a colored band.

• **Gift Services.** If your item would make a suitable gift, you can use this option to add a small icon to your listing of a gift-wrapped package. With Gift Services, you can offer any of these features: gift wrap, gift card, express shipping, and shipping to a gift recipient. Remember to explain these options in your item description and list any additional fees you charge.

- **Item Subtitle.** Adding a subtitle to your listing lets you add important descriptive words and phrases that buyers will see under your title while viewing search results or browsing categories. For example, if you're listing a camcorder with some additional equipment, your subtitle could be "Includes carrying case and 10 blank tapes." According to eBay, listings with subtitles are 18 percent more likely to sell.

- **Bold.** Bold makes your listing stand out among other listings using plain text. According to eBay's research, items with bold titles sell for 25 percent more than comparable listings. So if you expect your item to sell for more than $10, the bold feature is likely a wise investment.

- **Featured Plus.** This option gives your listing priority placement in the Featured Items section of the category list. Also, your item is emphasized at the top of the search results pages.

- **Pro Pack.** This option gives you a combined package of other listing upgrades at a discount. You receive Bold, Border, Highlight, Gallery Featured and Featured Plus.

- **Home Page Featured.** Your listing has a chance to rotate into a display on eBay's home page, although this is not guaranteed. Your item gets placement in eBay's Featured Items section. For most items you'll be selling, it's very, very, unlikely that the Home Page upgrade will be worth it.

- **10-day Duration.** This feature allows you to obtain the longest exposure for your listing for a nominal extra fee.

- **Listing Designer.** This feature enables you to create a professional-looking listing by adding themes and layouts without knowing HTML coding.

- **Scheduled Listings.** This allows you to list items up to three weeks in advance and control exactly when they begin and end. To schedule a listing, on the Sell Your Item form, select a start time from the Scheduled pull-down menu of **How you're selling.**

The best time to list

You'll increase your odds of selling at a good price by timing your auction so it's seen by the greatest possible number of eBay buyers. The busiest time on eBay is Sunday evening, simply because more people are at home with some spare time. Television ratings are generally better on Sunday nights, and so are the results on eBay.

Try to schedule your auctions to end between 5 p.m. and 9 p.m. on Sundays. Activity on eBay tails off on Monday evenings, then begins rising again on Thursdays.

There are exceptions. Consider the likely buyers of your item. If your market is teenagers, you might want to end your auction on a weeknight instead of a Friday night, when many teens are distracted by after-school activities and dates. If your likely buyer is a business customer, it's best to time your auction to end during a Tuesday afternoon, when the buyer is likely to be in the office and near a computer.

Avoid ending your auctions on holidays or during big events like the Super Bowl. When most people are outside their usual routine, they probably won't be shopping on eBay.

The news service AuctionBytes has an interactive auction calendar that can help you schedule your listings:

http://www.auctionbytes.com/cab/pages/calendar

Top 10 reasons your auction stinks

By Jim Cockrum

Want more bids on your auctions? Even though there are 1.5 billion page views per month on eBay, you still have to do several things right to attract bidders. Here are the most common reasons some auctions gather dust:

1. **You're in the wrong category.** While it's true that most shoppers on eBay use keyword searches to find what they're looking for, more and more shoppers are using the category search feature. This means you

must have your item in the correct category when launching your auction. To quickly determine what category is best, search for items similar to yours, and see what eBay category was used by those sellers. The assigned category of any auction item is always at the top of the listing auction just below the 10-digit item number.

2. **Your auction is ugly.** You don't have to be an artist with a college degree in marketing, but pay attention to your auction's appearance. Consider the overall color scheme and layout to improve your results. If you don't use HTML or pictures in your auctions already, it's time to start.

3. **It's unclear what you're selling.** For nearly any item you're selling, you'll need a nice photo in your listing. That's the best way to make it obvious to shoppers what is for sale. Be descriptive in your listing and tell the reader **immediately** what they're buying. Don't distract buyers with cute animations or musical effects in your auction listings.

4. **Your feedback rating is too low or negative.** If you are new to eBay and still have a (0) next to your eBay ID, it means you don't have any feedback yet. You can get some feedback and experience by buying anything (and paying for it) or by selling some in-demand items. Each transaction provides the opportunity to give and receive feedback. Too much negative feedback is a **huge** red flag to most buyers.

5. **Your item is not in demand.** Before listing anything on eBay, check the completed auctions for the same item. What was the final bid on the successful auctions? This helps you determine the likely results. If nobody else is selling what you have, there could be a very good reason: Nobody buys it.

6. **Your item is off-season.** Christmas items don't sell in July (except to bargain sharks).

7. **Your title is lousy.** You have to fill your title with vivid, descriptive keywords. "WOW" and "L@@K" are not good keywords. Don't use keywords that intentionally mislead or oversell your item. You may get more attention than you bargained for.

8. **Your shipping policies are vague.** Put yourself in the bidders' shoes. They want to know when and how their purchase will arrive. In competing with other sellers, your job is to be the "path of least resistance." Make everything easy for your customer. Make sure the customer understands as clearly as possible what the final total will be in addition to their bid. Whenever possible, offer **free shipping**. The increased bids will more than cover your shipping costs.

9. **You have unclear or few payment options.** Offer your customers as many payment options as possible. PayPal is preferred by most buyers, so you'll have fewer bidders and lower selling prices if you don't accept PayPal.

10. **Your opening price is too high.** Consider listing with the lowest possible opening bid. Many of my most successful auctions started with an opening bid of 1 cent. This often creates a bidding frenzy. Once a bidder places even the smallest bid on your item, they begin receiving e-mail reminders from eBay whenever they're outbid. This is automatic, free advertising for you. Remember, it's an auction! Start the bidding low!

A popular Internet marketing and auction expert, Cockrum is author of The Silent Sales Machine Hiding on eBay *and* How to Turn Auction Traffic into Cash. *For more information and to subscribe to Jim's free newsletter, see http://www.SilentJim.com.*

Use My eBay

My eBay is a central place on eBay's Web site where you can view all your selling and buying activity. There's a link to My eBay at the top of every eBay page. There you can manage your settings for selling, payments, e-mail and other features:

- **Set Notification preferences.** Determine how and when eBay sends you alerts or notifications.

- **Set Seller preferences.** Manage your settings for picture hosting, receiving payments, shipping, and other features.

- **Set Member-to-Member Communication preferences.**
  Specify whether buyers can contact you via Skype.

- **Set General preferences.** Adjust displays for recently viewed
  items and searches, My eBay preferences, third-party authoriza-
  tions, keeping yourself signed in, and showing your buyers' e-mail
  addresses with User IDs.

Even if selling on eBay isn't your full-time occupation, it's a good
idea to check for new announcements and messages at My eBay on a
daily basis. You'll find new opportunities and early warnings of potential problems. Pick a time of the day— first thing in the morning, or
perhaps lunchtime—to check in at My eBay.

Profit with a niche

Are you an expert on vintage board games? Antique clocks? Used printers? Consider making this your eBay specialty. The more you deal with a certain type of item, the better you'll learn how to find it at a bargain and resell it profitably.

Perhaps you already have a hobby or interest that would make a good eBay niche. Or perhaps it will occur to you a few months after getting your feet wet on eBay. But once you begin focusing on your niche, the more proficient you'll be in recognizing valuable items for resale and in locating new sources of inventory. You'll learn the market better than other sellers, and you'll benefit from repeat business from your satisfied customers.

- **Start with used merchandise.** Selling used items is a good way to gain experience on eBay without risking lots of cash. It's easy to find bargains at yard sales by snapping up the right books, clothing, glassware, electronics, or magazines. To be sure, building an inventory of used items is more laborious than buying new products from a wholesaler—with used items, you've got to drive from sale to sale, then haggle over items. But your profit margins are usually higher with used merchandise, and you can start small.

You can start gathering merchandise from your own attic, basement or closet. Used clothes, books, or even unwanted gifts can bring you valuable sales, feedback, and experience on eBay. Some items in particular can prove valuable:

- Old radios, stereos and electronic equipment. Don't assume that old cassette or 8-track tape player is worthless. eBay is populated by all sorts of collectors, and you might be surprised how much some of your old "junk" is worth.

- Old sports equipment such as fishing rods, baseball bats, basketballs, exercise devices and uniforms.

- Unused wedding, anniversary and birthday gifts. Turn that deadwood into cash and build your track record on eBay.

- Old books, videos, CDs and video games you don't plan to use anymore. Out-of-print items are particularly valuable.

- Old clothes, bathing suits, and shoes. Everything comes back into style sooner or later, and "vintage" clothing has never been hotter.

- Contents of thrift shops and charity marts run by Goodwill, Salvation Army, etc. Can you make good money by marking up the items you find at these shops and reselling them on eBay? Sure, and the stores are grateful for each dollar you spend there, which helps fund their programs.

Win with niche selling

By Skip McGrath

In the early days, you could sell just about anything on eBay and make money. Today, there's a lot more competition. Large eBay sellers have established businesses. Meanwhile, major corporations such as J.C. Penney, Bloomingdale's, and Disney have moved onto eBay in a big way.

The good news is, you don't have to sell the latest digital camera, Gucci shoes, or expensive diamond jewelry to make money on eBay. Some of the most profitable eBay sellers get their inventory from garage sales, thrift stores, flea markets, and closeout dealers. You can, too.

It's still possible for small sellers to make big profits. Your surest bet is to specialize. Seek out the offbeat and find used items that are in demand. Forget trying to sell computers, digital cameras, iPods and plasma TVs. There is no way you can compete with the big guys unless you have tons of money. And those drop-ship Web sites and programs that claim to have those products are mostly scams. Find a small niche—or several small niches that you can dominate.

The list of possible niche categories is virtually endless: used radio tubes, used (vintage) hi-fi equipment and parts, juggling supplies, used music and game CDs, old board games (Monopoly, Scrabble, etc.), clown equipment and supplies, used tools, old garden tools and decorative items, used college textbooks, small appliances (blenders, pasta machines, irons, etc.) personalized children's books, collectible fountain pens, new and used magic tricks and magic supplies, used bubble-pak and Styrofoam peanuts. The list goes on.

Along with being in a superior position to take advantage of repeat business, the benefits from becoming specialized are endless. If you know more about your product area, you will be able to buy at better prices and people who sense you specialize in something will be more comfortable buying from you.

Find your own niche. Define your market. Then you can know the type of person you're going to be selling to and the types of product you want to sell. You will also have less competition.

Search Listings on eBay to see what is selling. Go to: http://listings.eBay.com to see what is being listed and sold on eBay. The number in parentheses after the category title is the number of auctions for a given item. In general, the higher the number the more action and sales.

Become an expert in your field. Become an authority on what you do in your online auction business. If you sell printer ink cartridges, you want to be thought of before anyone else. When you become an authority in your field, a whole new universe of business and opportunity is opened up to you. I buy certain types of things on eBay from the same sellers over and over. I wouldn't dare do business with anyone else, not when my trusted buyers have proven themselves and their product. You want to earn that same type of position in the minds of eBayers for your niche.

Your niche category strategy

OK, you've put a lot of thought into your product and completed the introspective phase of getting started. You are excited about your merchandise and ready to start selling it. The next step is to find your niche market; as applied to online auctions, this refers to the category you will list your item(s) in. Considering eBay has more than 7,500 categories to choose from, this should be a relatively easy process. But there is one important strategic trick you should know.

Before listing your item in any category, follow these simple steps: First, browse through the eBay categories and write down the ones you feel are relevant to your product. You should be able to find at least 3-5 possible choices. Next, write down the number of auctions currently online in each of those categories (it will appear next to the category name). An average category has about 4,000, so if there are more than that you may conclude that the category is active. If there are less than 2,000 you may consider it inactive. I consider categories with more than 5,000 auctions to be popular, and those with over 10,000 are most popular. Some categories have more than 50,000 auctions going at any one time. Using this ranking system, rate the categories that you have chosen for your product.

I recommend listing in the most active categories only because they get the most traffic. If you put your product in an inactive section of eBay, you may get few or no bids, even if you feature it. Avoid categories with fewer than 1,000 auctions online unless your product is highly specialized to that category!

A longtime eBay PowerSeller, McGrath publishes "The eBay Sellers Resource Site" at http://www.skipmcgrath.com, where you can subscribe to a free newsletter for professional eBay sellers. He is the author of several best-selling eBay how-to books, including "Three Weeks to eBay Profits," "Titanium eBay," and "How to Start and Run an eBay Consignment Business."

Cash in on collectibles

Even if you don't set out to deal in collectibles, once you've been selling for a while, you're bound to run into some special items. When that happens, don't shirk the extra research required to describe and price your gems properly.

Autographed items. Items that are signed by celebrities often fetch great prices, but such items are easily forged. For this reason, signed items are often sold with a "Certificate of Authenticity" (COA), which reassures buyers that the signature was really made by the advertised person.

But COAs can be forged just as easily as autographs. For this reason it's important to research the "authenticator" who signed the COA. Many are reputable, and many are not. eBay maintains a list of authenticators it recommends, and those who are unacceptable. See:

http://pages.ebay.com/help/policies/autographs.html

To prevent misunderstandings between buyers and sellers of signed items, include the following details in auctions of autographed items:

- A good-quality photo of the autographed item.

- All pertinent details from the COA (if there is one), especially the name of the person or company, who issued the certificate, and a scanned image of the COA.

- Refund policy. Seller should offer refunds in the event that a reputable dealer discovers that the autograph is fake.

Trust, but authenticate

Using an authentication service. In cases where you believe your item is of sufficient value, you may wish to consult a professional appraiser or an authentication service. Consult your local Yellow Pages or visit the International Society of Appraisers: **http://www.isa-appraisers.org/**

Also, eBay maintains a list of recommended appraisers who are skilled in identifying a variety of different items. These appraisers serve both eBay buyers and sellers, but promise not to buy or sell on eBay, which prevents them from competing with the buyers and sellers using their services.

You might also obtain an appraisal for $9.95 from the "What it's Worth to You" service:

http://www.whatsitworthtoyou.com/

How to recognize fake autographs

By Ken Zajac

Perhaps no other detail adds as much instant value to a collectible as a signature. Yet nothing is easier for scammers to fake, or harder for beginners to authenticate. Here are some tips:

- **Watch out** for felt-pen signatures, a common trick. It's easy to fake a signature using a felt pen. But felt-tip pens weren't sold until the 1960s, so an ink pen must have been used if the signature is older than 1960.

- **Cut signatures** are risky. Anything cut away from the rest of a document may be a fake or a printed signature, or taken from a reproduction. It was popular during the 1976 U.S. Bicentennial to sell reproductions of famous documents made on onion paper, which looks old but isn't. Some unscrupulous sellers purchase complete repros just to cut the printed signatures out and try to sell them as autographs.

- **Watch out** for signed index cards; most aren't real. If you were a president, for example, would you sign your name over and over on common index cards?

- **Beware of** signed baseballs, especially if the signature is of a political figure—most of these are printed or stamped. Think about it—can anyone sign their name on a curved surface to make it appear just like their signature on a flat piece of paper?

- **Often**, "signed" items are printed or made with an auto-pen. The majority of John F. Kennedy signatures are autopens or printed, as are Jacqueline Kennedy's name on thousands of replies to condolence letters after JFK's assassination. The familiar, official White House photos of JFK and Jackie all have printed signatures. Even letters from Kennedy's secretary, Evelyn Lincoln, were often printed.

- Letters written by famous political figures are usually signed by an auto-pen unless it's a **personal** letter.

- **Photos** of famous figures usually contain a signature that was printed as part of the photo. Books are a common source of photos that were printed with authentic-looking autographs.

- Computers make the forgery of autographed photos easier than ever. A general rule of thumb: If the photo is **glossy** and the subject is dated, it's probably a modern copy. Glossy photo paper has only become common in recent decades.

Zajac is an antiques dealer in Tacoma, Wash.

Get more great inventory

Selling used items is a great way to start on eBay. The profit margins on used items can be extremely healthy once you learn how to spot potentially valuable items.

To efficiently find items that can be resold profitably, you'll need sources in your area where you can regularly find a variety of items at reasonable prices. Here's where to start:

- **Estate sales.** Estate sales can be a reliable source of fine, bargain-priced items. Usually advertised in newspaper ads, these sales liquidate the entire contents of a household, and can include large groups of used items, collectibles, and unused gifts.

If you attend an estate sale, plan on being the first in the door. This can mean standing in line for 45 minutes or more at a well-publicized sale, but getting first crack at the contents can be worth the wait.

Most estate sales are held on Friday or Saturday mornings. Larger sales may begin on Thursday and continue through Sunday. Remaining items are usually marked down 50 percent on the last day, so a good sale may be worth a second visit. But don't pass up good items on Friday or Saturday because you think you'll get them more cheaply on Sunday. By then, 98 percent of the cream will be skimmed. Get the good stuff while you can.

If there are more estate sales advertised on a given Saturday than you have time to attend, it's worth doing some detective work to determine which sales are likely to have the best items. The newspaper ad should have a contact number for the liquidator running the sale. Phone ahead and ask what types of merchandise are available. Don't rely on the newspaper ad, which might prominently mention "oil paintings," for example, when only a few cheap reproductions are for sale. And it never fails, the advertisement won't mention the most valuable items being sold.

If estate sales work well for you, it's worthwhile to cultivate a relationship with the estate liquidators who work in your area. Leave your business card and ask to be notified of all upcoming sales. These contacts may also be able to alert you to collections that come up for sale outside the estate liquidation process. Likewise, familiarize yourself with local funeral directors and estate attorneys, who can alert you to good opportunities.

- **Bankruptcy sales.** When businesses or shops go out of business, often their merchandise and office equipment is auctioned off. The sales are sometimes advertised in the local newspapers. Sometimes you can get word of these sales through local bankruptcy attorneys or the clerk of your county's bankruptcy court. It can take some work to learn the proper procedures for getting access to bankruptcy auctions, but it can result in big opportunities.

Sometimes the contents of storage facilities, where people store excess household items, are auctioned or sold off. Every month, a certain number of storage units must be cleared out by companies like Public Storage when the contents are left unclaimed and the owner quits paying storage fees. Sometimes these sales are advertised, but it doesn't hurt to ask local storage companies to notify you of these opportunities.

- **Garage sales** and **yard sales**. Weekend neighborhood sales can be a good source of stock if you enjoy wheeling and dealing. Garage and yard sales require lots of legwork, though, and the proportion of junk to gems can be high.

The main problem is that these sales are full of the stuff people no longer want, in contrast with an estate sale that liquidates the entire contents of a household. Some yard salers have caught on to this difference and now advertise their garage sales as "estate sales," aiming to draw more buyers. When you're scanning the classifieds, beware of yard sales masquerading as estate sales. An "estate sale" that does not advertise items like antique furniture, silver, and stemware might be a yard sale in disguise.

- **Thrift shops.** Thrift shops can be worthwhile sources of merchandise, particularly when the items are mispriced. Sometimes items are worth more online than in a physical store. Church thrift shops are a potential source of stock too. The prices are usually reasonable and the donated items are sometimes of higher quality than those at commercial thrift shops.

- **Local artisans.** One good way to obtain products is to find local artists, painters, potters, rug makers, and others who may have unique, interesting products you can sell online. If the products are unusual, it's likely that no other eBay sellers will have similar merchandise, and your profits should be healthy. One disadvantage is that hand-made items are produced slowly, so you may have trouble finding enough items to build a high-volume business.

If you or a family member has a creative hobby, you can consider selling those items or services on eBay too. eBay is a fantastic opportunity for artists and craftsmen to sell their wares directly to the public, without having to sell at huge discounts to galleries or stores.

- **Close-out merchandise.** Local retail stores have only a certain amount of time to sell items they're carrying. At some point, the remaining items (such as winter clothing or last year's stereo equipment) are marked down for clearance, perhaps at more than 50 percent off.

In some stores, this clearance merchandise may be displayed in tables in the front of the store. If you talk to the store's manager, you can often get this clearance merchandise for even less—and you may find out about other bargains stuck in the back room.

You're in a strong bargaining position if you can offer to haul off a quantity of merchandise. If a store can't move clearance items fast enough, the retailer might have to sell it to a liquidator for 10 percent to 15 percent of retail. You can probably offer a bit more than the liquidators. For example, by getting the goods at 80 percent off retail, and reselling it on eBay at 40 percent off retail, you're making a healthy profit.

Factory stores and outlet mall stores fall into this same general category. Their merchandise turns over rapidly, presenting a constant stream of opportunities.

One note of caution: Don't gamble on a large quantity of merchandise without researching to see how much it's selling for on eBay. If there's no demand for the stuff, it doesn't matter if you get it for 99 percent off retail. It will still be dead money.

• **Library sales.** For acquiring used books, library sales are hard to beat. Sales are often conducted monthly, usually on a Saturday, and feature a wide variety of books at very low prices. Most library sales are organized by a nonprofit Friends of the Library (FOL) group, and most of the books for sale are donated by area residents in very good or like-new condition. Because the library can't absorb most of this material into its collection, the surplus is offered for public sale as a fundraiser. Nearly all the books are priced at a dollar or two apiece, and again, lots of them can be sold for $10 or more online. Everything from current bestsellers to antique volumes is likely to be on sale. You'll likely find some videos and CDs at these sales too.

Many libraries also have a small daily book sale at a shelf or cart near the lobby, and some larger library systems even operate a full-time used bookstore. Sometimes these stores, tucked away in a library basement, are unadvertised gold mines.

In addition to libraries, schools and civic groups organize book sales, and these sales can include some high-quality donated stock.

• **Overstock distributors.** New items that have been returned from retail stores can be a profitable source of inventory. In this case, you're buying from the liquidators that have already cleared merchandise from retailers. If you buy the right items, this can be a good sideline to your used-merchandise business, expanding your volume and profits. You can get identical items in quantity, and re-use the same photos and descriptions for subsequent listings, saving time. However, the average profit margin will be probably be lower than for used items. Be careful to avoid buying items that are already in plentiful supply on eBay because price competition among sellers can eliminate your profits.

Find overlooked gems at estate sales
By John Landahl

Follow these tips and learn to find overlooked gems at estate and yard sales you can resell on eBay for big markups.

- Look for items that date from the 1970s or earlier, are in good condition, and are still in their original boxes. Seek nostalgia items that Baby Boomers in their 40s and 50s remember from childhood. Lunchboxes, toys, home décor items, hand tools, and games are but a few examples.

- Concentrate on small vintage items still in their original boxes. Small items are easiest to carry, store, pack, and ship. The original box gives important information about the manufacturer and the precise item name to use in your eBay description. For collectors, the box adds significant value.

- If in doubt, pick it up. If you leave an interesting item sitting while you ponder it, someone else will snatch it. Possession is nine-tenths of the law!

- Think twice about items with no identifying name or manufacturer. For example, generic ceramics are difficult to sell on eBay because buyers searching for name brands won't find them.

- Be careful with film cameras or other gadgets that are hard to test. Faulty electronic gear results in lots of returns and negative feedback.

- Selling fine artwork on eBay is tough unless you're an expert. Artists' popularity comes and goes, and authenticating pieces can be more trouble than it's worth.

- Large, bulky or fragile items are a nightmare to pack and ship. If you're in doubt, don't buy that sculpture unless you'd enjoy seeing it on your own mantelpiece—it might end up there.

- Don't overbuy. Remember, each item you acquire must be carefully researched, photographed, described, and weighed. You'll spend time answering e-mails from prospective buyers. And if the item sells, you've got to pack and ship it.

- Discriminate. Set a buying budget and stick to it. If you buy everything in sight, you'll lose money because you'll end up with too many unsold duds.

- Buy cheap unless you're certain of the value. Buying several items for $10 apiece is much safer than buying a single $50 item.

- Remember, there's always another sale. What you'll find at the next one is completely unpredictable.

- The more sales you can hit in one trip, the better. Be efficient and plan your route. Use an Internet mapping service like MapQuest or Google Maps to plot the location of your sales.

- Search Internet classified services such as CraigsList.com to find more sales not listed in the newspaper.

  Landahl is author of "Estate Sale Prospecting for Fun and Profit with CraigsList and eBay."

Live auctions

Scan your daily newspapers for notices of local auctions. You'll find news of estate auctions, bankruptcy auctions, and sometimes auctions dealing with specific types of merchandise or office equipment.

The right merchandise bought at a local auction can often be sold for triple your cost on eBay. Why? Well, let's imagine that you attend an auction this weekend in a nearby town. You buy a box of old comic books for $20. Just a few comics collectors attended the auction, since it was advertised only in the local paper. However, when you list the comics on eBay, you're offering them simultaneously to thousands of collectors. Once two or more bidders decide they want those comics, competition raises the price, creating more interest in your merchandise. And you could end up selling those comics on eBay for $150 or more.

You can do the same thing with practically any type of auctioned merchandise, such as antique furniture, toys, books, artwork, or other collectibles. The more practice you get at this, the better you'll recognize what sells on eBay, and where the bargains are at local auctions.

- **Postal Service auctions.** The U.S. Postal Service conducts public auctions at mail "recovery centers" around the country to liquidate unclaimed, damaged, and claim-paid merchandise. The lots vary in size, but tend to be large and heavy.

Most of the items in Postal Service auctions are like-new or brand-new items that have simply come unpackaged and separated from the delivery address in the mail. However, the auctions are potluck—sometimes there's no list of the exact contents, which can include miscellaneous items. The value of the individual items can range from practically nothing to hundreds of dollars. These auctions can present good buys, but whether it is worth your while will depend on what is included in the lot and how high the bidding goes.

For details on upcoming Postal Service auctions, check this Web page:

www.usps.com/auctions

In addition to auctions, the Postal Service occasionally conducts sales of personal property or its own equipment. These sales are conducted at local post offices and are advertised in local newspapers.

- **Treasury Department auctions.** The U.S. Customs Service regularly auctions off property it has seized for trade violations, trademark or copyright violations, smuggling, drug trafficking, money laundering, and other crimes. The auctioned property includes all sorts of items and sometimes includes large lots of consumer merchandise and even motor vehicles, airplanes and boats.

Most Customs auctions are conducted in New Jersey, Texas, California, and Arizona. It's possible to get a good buy on merchandise at these sales, but as is the case with any auction, the final price for items depends on public interest and what people are willing to pay for them. It's a good idea to go early and inspect the merchandise. Payment is due at the auction. For more information, see the Treasury Department's Web site:

www.treas.gov/auctions

• **GSA Auctions.** The U.S. government's General Services Administration runs a Web-based auction system allowing registered participants to bid on a single item or bulk lots. GSA Auctions offer federal personal property ranging from commonplace items like office equipment and furniture to more specialized items like scientific equipment, heavy machinery, aircraft, boats and other vehicles. Through the Web site, the GSA allows buyers across the country to bid on and buy any of the offered items. See:

http://www.gsa.gov/Portal/gsa/ep/contentView.do?contentId=9881&contentType=GSA_BASIC

• **Government Liquidation.** This is an online marketplace that sells U.S. government surplus and scrap material to the public. The site offers more than 500 commodity categories and thousands of surplus items are added weekly. The U.S. Defense Department sells items through Government Liquidation, which also runs the Web site Liquidation.com. See:

http://www.govliquidation.com

- **Law enforcement auctions.** Local police agencies often sell used equipment and recovered stolen property. There are many Web sites that advertise police auctions, but you can also find out about upcoming sales by simply calling your local police department. Ask if you can be put on a mail or e-mail list so you'll be notified of future sales. Check the classified section of your local newspaper for announcements and the Web sites **PoliceAuctions.com** and **PropertyRoom.com.**

- **Classified ads.** If you have trouble finding enough stock using the sources discussed above, try placing a classified advertisement yourself: "Cash paid for your used items."

If you place an ad offering to pay people cash, you'd better be ready for a response. The challenge is keeping the nuisance responses to a minimum. Don't give anyone the impression that you're itching to spend a wad of cash on any old junk. Keep expectations low. One strategy that seems to work is offering a "finder's fee" for referrals to a collection you agree to buy.

Ads in metropolitan daily newspapers are costly, so look for alternatives such as weekly newspapers and circulars like *Penny Saver* and *Thrifty Nickel*. Another option is CraigsList.com, the online classified service, which is free. The home page displays classified ads for the San Francisco Bay area, but you'll find a link to your nearest metro area.

While you're at it, don't overlook other free forms of local advertising, such as bulletin boards in local stores and community centers, and signs and posters.

Get merchandise on eBay

Some of the most successful eBay sellers get many of their items right on eBay. Regular sellers and some high-volume wholesalers are constantly listing auctions in many eBay categories. Each and every day there are hundreds of bulk lots of used and new merchandise listed on this section of eBay:

http://pages.ebay.com/catindex/catwholesale.html

One way you can save money with a wholesale lot is limiting your search to sellers in your area. That way you can inspect the goods before bidding and haul the merchandise yourself, saving on shipping.

Get merchandise on consignment

If enough people know you're an eBay seller, eventually someone may ask you to sell some of their items. And while consignment selling produces several unique challenges, it is a surefire way of expanding your business.

Consignment selling solves the main problem for someone starting a new online business: finding enough merchandise to sell at prices low enough to bring a profit. With the consignment model, people bring the merchandise to you, and after you sell it, you pocket a commission less your expenses. If it doesn't sell, you return the item to its owner.

The potential is huge with consignment selling. Think of the millions of people who are interested in getting cash for their old possessions, but don't have the initiative to sell on eBay themselves. Many of these folks probably realize they could get much higher prices for their items by letting someone else sell them on eBay, rather than holding a yard sale.

Pitfalls await the consignment seller, though. To do it right, you need to set up a real bookkeeping system. You'll need good insurance coverage if you store merchandise belonging to someone else, in the event of fire, flood, or some other disaster. There's also the problem of managing the expectations of the folks you're accepting merchandise from. Popular shows such as "Antiques Roadshow" have convinced too many people that treasures are lurking in their attic or basement. Lots of the stuff isn't valuable, it's just old. You don't want to be roped into babysitting someone else's junk.

Even more issues can confound the consignment seller, things that don't trouble the typical eBayer. For example, how can you represent yourself as a bonded auctioneer? How do you protect yourself from illegal activity such as selling stolen goods?

And perhaps the biggest consideration of all for potential consignment sellers: Are you a "people person?" Do you enjoy being around other people and getting input regarding your business from lots of different folks? If you are indeed a people person, you might find the business invigorating. On the other hand, if you're not, it might be a pain in the neck.

If you want to keep your business as simple and worry-free as possible, avoid consignment selling. If the items offered for consignment look good to you, offer to buy them outright. Sell them yourself and avoid the hassles of a consignment deal.

On the other hand, a consignment operation is the sort of business that can be scaled much larger, and opening an eBay "drop-off store" could be your long-term goal. To bolster your qualifications, you can sign up with eBay to become a "Trading Assistant" and be listed in their Web site directory, where potential customers can find you by ZIP Code (more details on this in the following section).

Some eBay drop-off stores average a commission rate of 40 percent. In other words, if an item sells for $100 after expenses, the seller pays the item's original owner $60, and pockets $40.

According to Skip McGrath, a longtime eBay PowerSeller and author of *How to Start and Run an eBay Consignment Business*, a one-person eBayer relatively skilled at selling could generate $1,000 to $5,000 in weekly profits by building a well-oiled consignment business. You could ramp up even bigger if you hired some employees and committed to rent payments and advertising.

Become a trading assistant

Once you're an experienced seller, you can offer your services to the public as an official eBay Trading Assistant, selling items as a service. As a Trading Assistant, you help others realize the benefits of selling their items on eBay without having to open their own accounts.

Many Trading Assistants sell on behalf of others as a way to supplement their regular eBay income. Whether you're a full-time or part-time Trading Assistant, you can run your business as you wish, specifying the types of items you deal with, your fees, and your hours of operation.

Once you're a Trading Assistant, you can be listed in eBay's directory, which can help in acquiring new business.

• **Getting new client leads.** Through the Trading Assistant Directory, your business is marketed on a global level. You can also drive additional marketing efforts by downloading flier templates, press kits, and program logos. You can also take advantage of the variety of training and education opportunities, including the TA Education & Training hub and TA Workshops.

• **Trading Assistant requirements.** To be included in the Trading Assistant Directory and have access to Trading Assistant marketing materials, you must have sold an average of four items per month during the previous three months, and have a feedback score of 100 or higher with at least 97 percent positive feedback.

For more info on eBay's Trading Assistant Program, see:

http://pages.ebay.com/tahub/already.html

Expand your business

eBay sellers with at least $1,000 per month in sales who maintain a positive feedback rate of at least 98 percent can receive PowerSeller status. These members receive a special icon beside their User IDs, get priority access to telephone support, a special discussion board, and a few other perks.

There's no mystery about how to achieve PowerSeller status. Just keep doing the things that are effective for you. Be as efficient as possible and you can constantly expand your business. Here are more principles to keep in mind:

- **Sell "lots" to keep your average sale higher.** As your eBay business gets bigger, you'll need to become more efficient in the way you locate new merchandise, list it, and ship it. One great way to streamline your administrative tasks is to sell "lots" of items instead of individual pieces whenever possible. For example, let's imagine you have six sweaters, all the same size but different colors. You can probably find one buyer for all six. And selling everything in one auction makes your operation more efficient in several important ways:

  - You ship all the items to a single buyer. You collect payment, ship, and communicate with one buyer instead of several.

  - You spend less time listing the individual items for sale. There are fewer eBay fees and less to keep track of.

  - It's likely that one or two of the sweaters wouldn't have sold individually. Selling them as a group ensures that you move out this merchandise and make room for new items.

Create your 'About Me' page

Once you're serious about eBay, publishing an "About Me" page is a no-brainer. It's a personal Web page you can use to let the rest of the community know more about you. You can add a personal touch or keep it strictly business. You might display some of your prized listings, describe your hobbies, and display a picture or two of yourself or your pets. Letting some personality shine through on your About Me page helps your past customers remember you, and helps prospective customers get comfortable with you. Also, if you have another business outside eBay, you can link to it here.

You can use HTML code or select a pre-formatted format for your page. You'll be able to preview your About Me page, then click **Submit** to publish it. You can always go back and edit your About Me page if you like. You can change the format, add or remove pictures, or delete the page entirely.

If you don't have your own Web site, the URL of your About Me page is a good addition to your business cards and e-mail signature. You can include links to your About Me page in your listings.

You can view the About Me page for any eBay member by clicking the **Me** icon next to the User ID.

Cross-promotions

• Cross-promoting your eBay items is one of your best tools for selling additional merchandise to your buyers. When buyers bid or buy one of your items, four of your other items are displayed. Combining this feature with an offer of a shipping discount for additional purchases is a strong incentive for buyers to purchase more items from you simultaneously.

By default, buyers see your cross-promotions during checkout. Cross-promotions are also displayed when a buyer visits one of your eBay Store listings. However, it's not mandatory for sellers to use cross-promotions—you can out of this feature by changing your preferences in My eBay.

- **Fine-tune your cross-promotions.** Cross-promotions are more powerful if you promote certain items in the right situation. You can create "rules" for your cross-promotions to make them more effective. For example, you can stipulate that whenever a buyer bids on a tennis racquet, tennis balls are promoted too. Store sellers can also set how many items appear in cross-promotion displays (a maximum of 12) and other preferences.

Here's how to set your cross-promotion preferences:

- In My eBay, click **Marketing Tools.**
- Click **Settings** under Cross Promotions.
- Set preferences.

Open an eBay store

When you have a sufficient inventory and you decide to concentrate on developing your eBay business further, you should consider expanding your business by opening an eBay Store. The requirements are simple: You'll need to have a feedback score of 20 or more, be ID Verified, or have a PayPal account in good standing.

eBay's Store listing fees are much lower than auction fees, making a Store a good place to park merchandise between auctions, to clear slow-moving merchandise, and to provide a browsing destination for your previous customers. You can put a clickable link into your Store within your regular eBay auctions.

If you put some effort into your eBay Store, you'll probably make back the $15.95 monthly subscription fee several times over. For example, you might run a promotion at your Store in which you offer free shipping to customers who buy at least two items. Or you might offer a 35 percent markdown on all your items to spark sales during the "dog days" of summer.

The Store Inventory listing format is fixed-price. Listings have a longer duration and lower insertion fees. Store items get less exposure than auctions because Store listings usually don't show up in eBay search results. You can create Store listings by using eBay's Sell Your Item Form and other listing tools.

Three Store subscription levels are available: basic at $15.95 a month, premium at $49.95 a month, and anchor at $299.95 a month. For a rundown on the features of each subscription level, see:

http://pages.ebay.com/storefronts/subscriptions.html

Set up shop

Once you decide which level of Store subscription is right for you, you have the option of using the "Quick Store Setup" to customize your Store. This feature recommends design and marketing features that have worked well for other sellers. You can apply the recommended settings or edit them to suit your situation. If you change your mind later, you can use the **Manage My Store** feature in My eBay to change any Store settings.

You can customize your Store with your favorite colors, images, and text styles, and you can create up to 300 categories and subcategories for your items.

● **Name your store.** You can use your eBay User ID as your Store name or you can select a different name. The name determines your store's Web address, the URL. For example, if your Store's name is "Car Parts," your Store's URL is **http://stores.ebay.com/car-parts**. eBay automatically adds hyphens between words, makes all letters lower case, and deletes "special" characters such as apostrophes and spaces.

Try to pick a name that tells buyers something about your inventory. A specific name like "Baseball Hats" works better than a vague name like "Perry's Picks," which doesn't help buyers understand what's for sale. Also, by using descriptive words, search engines like

Google will help people find your Store, even if they weren't shopping on eBay to begin with.

Some Store names are prohibited by eBay. You can't use a name containing the words eBay, Half.com or PayPal. You can't use a name identical to or very similar to any trademark or someone else's company name. Your Store name can't contain the characters **www** or end with a domain abbreviation such as .com, .net or .biz.

You can change your name at any time, but should avoid doing so because any existing bookmarks or Web links to your Store will quit working. At Google and other search engines, your Store will be considered a new site, and you'll lose any ranking you had.

Promote your store

Unlike regular eBay auctions and fixed-price listings, your Store listings won't be as visible to browsers, so to get sales you must draw people into your Store. One way sellers can attract buyers to their Stores is by linking to them in their regular auctions and fixed-price listings. You can include links to your Store items in your regular item descriptions. You can link to your Store's home page, categories, or specific items.

You can also have Store items appear in your cross-promotion displays.

eBay offers a variety of marketing tools for Store operators, including e-mail marketing. Access these tools from My eBay by clicking on **Marketing Tools**.

To generate more traffic to your store, mention your Store URL on your packing slips, business cards, advertisements, e-mail signatures, and other promotional materials.

- **e-Mail Marketing.** E-mail newsletters are an efficient way to promote your eBay store to previous customers and members who have expressed an interest in your store but haven't bought anything yet. To access this feature:

    - Click **My eBay** at the top of any eBay page.

- In the left column, click **Marketing Tools.**

- Under **Store Marketing**, click **Email Marketing**.

Buyers can ask to receive your e-mail newsletter when they add you to their **Favorite Sellers** list or by clicking **Sign Up to Store Newsletter.**

Using eBay's Web site, you create your e-mail newsletter with links to your Store items. You can specify which subscribers receive an e-mail based on their interests and buying history.

You can create as many as five mailing lists to advertise different promotions or target different interests. For example, you could have a "Baseball Cards" mailing list and a "Weekly Sale" mailing list.

After sending your newsletters, you'll be able to gauge their effectiveness by viewing statistics on the number of resulting bids and Buy It Now transactions.

Depending on your Store subscription level, you're allocated a certain number of free monthly e-mails. For example, Basic Stores get 5,000 free e-mails and can purchase more for 1 cent apiece.

- **Promotional fliers.** You can easily print a promotional flier to publicize your eBay Store. You might highlight new items, promote special deals, and remind buyers of your return policy and how to leave feedback. You can enclose your fliers in shipments to buyers, hand them out to friends and acquaintances, and tack them to bulletin boards. To begin:

- Click **My eBay** at the top of any eBay page.

- Click **Marketing Tools** in the left-hand column.

- Click **Promotional Flyer** in the left-hand column.

- **Shipping Discounts.** Offering shipping discounts on multiple purchases is a proven method of getting buyers to purchase more items. Many buyers who might have quit after purchasing just one item will take the time to browse your entire inventory once they see an offer for free shipping.

When you offer shipping discounts, buyers see the message **Save on shipping** in your listing. When buyers pay for more than one item, eBay automatically figures the shipping discount and subtracts it from their total shipping fee. The discount is shown to buyers when they pay.

You can set your shipping discounts in your My eBay **Preferences**.

• **Have a sale at your Store.** Having an occasional sale is a great way to jump-start sales. You can create sales linked to seasons or specific holidays, categories of merchandise, or just as a clearance event.

eBay's **Markdown Manager** automates this process for you. You can discount your listings by a percentage or by price. You can apply discounts to part or all of your Store inventory, and promote your sale with e-mail marketing. See:

http://pages.ebay.com/storefronts/markdownmanager.html

• **eBay Express**. In 2006 eBay launched a new section of its Web site called eBay Express. It emphasizes fixed-price listings, not auctions. Certain eBay items—mostly new, fixed-price items—show up automatically on Express. Buyers use a shopping cart and can purchase from multiple sellers with one payment.

• **eBay Store traffic reports.** You'll have access to traffic reports from your eBay Store that show how visitors behave at your store, your listings, and other pages. You can discover which pages are viewed most often and which Web sites and search keywords bring in the most traffic for you. To view your traffic reports:

• From My eBay, click **Manage My Store.**

• Click **Traffic Reports.**

You must view your traffic reports at least once every 90 days, or the reports will stop.

- **Using eBay's Half.com site.** If your inventory includes standard media items such as books, music or video games, consider listing your items for sale at Half.com. All items are listed at fixed prices. Feedback you receive from buyers will show up in your eBay account, and vice versa.

Half.com charges sellers no fees for listing items, but takes a 15 percent commission on sales.

The payment procedures on Half.com differ from eBay. Instead of using PayPal, buyers pay directly with a credit card, and sellers receive their proceeds in a monthly check or online bank transfer.

- **Google Base.** Google offers free software enabling you to enhance your Store's visibility on the Web. The software, called "Google Base Store Connector," puts details about your inventory, called a "feed," into the search engine's index. Then when people search Google for products like yours, your listings show up along with a link to your site.

"This is the best thing I've come across yet for eBay store owners, and the absolute best part is it's totally free," said the eBay PowerSeller known as history-bytes. "Google has built a free tool to let you upload all of your auctions into it, so that hundreds of millions of customers worldwide can find your auctions—and buy them."

To find out more:

http://www.google.com/base/storeconnector/index.html

eBay also has an internal procedure enabling sellers to create a feed of their inventory. For more information on exporting a file of your eBay listings, see:

http://pages.ebay.com/help/specialtysites/exporting-your-listings.html

Why many would-be PowerSellers fail

By Skip McGrath

Hundreds of new eBay sellers crash and burn every month. Here are the most common mistakes you should avoid:

● **Poor Feedback Rating.** New eBay sellers typically underrate the importance of quickly building a great feedback rating. When starting your eBay business, you should bend over backwards to provide exceptional service. Remember, you're fishing for compliments. As the seller, you have a lot to lose from negative feedback. It's only a question of time until you run into a difficult or irrational buyer. He or she may be rude, or unresponsive, or both. While you're building your feedback rating, sometimes you just have to swallow hard and be extra-diplomatic. Once your feedback rating is established in the high hundreds, you can afford to fight back and absorb the occasional negative feedback without suffering a big hit to your average.

● **Not accepting credit cards turns away bidders.** Thousands of bidders worry about Internet fraud. Studies by eBay have firmly concluded that accepting credit cards increases your auction bids between 100 percent and 300 percent.

In the old days, it was tough for new, small merchants to get a card processing account, but PayPal offers an elegant solution. There are no set-up fees and transaction costs are 2.2 percent or less. By contrast, setting up an old-fashioned merchant card account can cost between $195 to $425 in setup fees and anywhere from 2.5 percent to 7.5 percent per transaction.

● **Weak headlines and poor auction descriptions lose bids.** To attract bidders, your headline must stand out above the competition. A great headline contains two key elements: "Keywords" that are searchable, and "emotional words" designed to draw attention. Before writing the auction description, ask yourself: "Why would someone want to own this item?" If you're selling something you used yourself, say so. Tell the potential bidder why you owned the item, how you used it, and what benefits it brought you. Sell not just the features, but the benefits and the romance.

- **Poor images turn off buyers.** The saying "a picture is worth a thousand words" is especially true at eBay. Not having a photo of your item will greatly reduce your bids and cause unprofitable or unsuccessful auctions. Not only must you have a photograph of your item, the photo must be accurate and revealing. It's not necessary to be a professional photographer. eBay bidders understand that most sellers are taking snapshots. But your photo should be clear, and show the product as completely as possible.

- **Not understanding your costs is a prescription for disaster.** It's easy for a new seller to get caught up in the excitement of selling and ignore the costs of selling. Before deciding whether to list something on eBay and what to sell it for (i.e. reserve or Dutch auction price), you must understand all the costs involved. First, there's the insertion fee, then, if it sells, the final-value fee. There may be a fee to process the payment. If you use an auction-management service such as Andale, don't forget their fees. Then there's shipping and the cost of packing materials. If you're selling items you purchased wholesale, you probably paid for the items to be shipped to you. Did you pay sales tax?

A longtime eBay PowerSeller, McGrath publishes "The eBay Sellers Resource Site" at http://www.skipmcgrath.com, where you can subscribe to a free newsletter for professional eBay sellers. He is the author of several best-selling eBay how-to books, including "Three Weeks to eBay Profits," Titanium eBay," and "How to Start and Run an eBay Consignment Business."

Prevent problem customers

Many eBay sellers like to think of themselves as retailers, but it's also helpful to consider your business as a *service*. You're selling convenience and service just as much as you're selling products. Most of your sales will come from new customers, and the only way to differentiate yourself from competitors is the "feedback" record you earn by providing good service to buyer after buyer.

- **Set Buyer Requirements.** If you do business with enough people, sooner or later you're going to run into someone you'd rather not deal with again. Fortunately, eBay allows you to block certain buyers from bidding on or buying your items based on whether they have a PayPal account, their country of registration, feedback, and buying history. Here's how to add buyer requirements to your listings:

  - From My eBay, in the My Account column, click **Preferences**.

  - In the Seller Preferences section, click **Edit.**

  - On the Buyer Requirements page, select your buyer requirements.

  - Click the **Submit** button to save your settings. You can also create a requirements exemption list.

Be a feedback fanatic

eBay's feedback system enables transaction partners who don't know each other to predict one another's likely performance. This facilitates trade because buyers can easily see the track record of sellers, and vice versa. Once you've earned a strong feedback record, you have a huge advantage over competing sellers and can even command higher prices.

eBay members receive one rating point from each transaction partner—positive, neutral or negative. A perfect feedback percentage score is 100, and careful sellers can expect to keep their positive feedback averages well above 90. eBay counts feedback from the same buyer only once; otherwise it would be possible for two people colluding to dramatically boost their feedback scores and give other buyers the impression of a longer trading history.

Transactions completed on Half.com also count toward your eBay feedback score.

Sellers gripe about feedback systems, which are always imperfect, but feedback can serve as a useful tool for managing your business. By aiming to minimize negative feedback, you'll automatically be focused on preventing mistakes that cost money to correct.

The best way to prevent bad feedback is to have a daily routine for managing your business. For example, morning can be a good time to check your messages and answer inquiries received overnight. Prompt communication with buyers prevents small problems from growing into big problems.

Having satisfied customers is fine, but the real payoff comes through future rewards of repeat sales. Satisfied customers come back again and again, and that's the lifeblood of every successful business.

You should take extreme care and exercise patience when leaving feedback ratings for buyers for a variety of reasons:

• It's a reflection on your business. Potential customers may review feedback ratings you've left for previous buyers.

- Feedback can't be edited or removed after it's posted. It becomes a permanent record on eBay and is visible to anyone, unless the transaction partners mutually agree to remove it or in the unlikely event that eBay removes it at your request.

- You could be held liable for legal damages to your buyer's reputation if a court found your statements were libelous or defamatory.

- eBay might restrict or suspend your account if it determines you've posted abusive feedback.

So to maintain your level of service and minimize negative feedback, focus on the things you can control: prompt shipping, careful communication, and accurate descriptions.

- **Detailed Seller Ratings.** In addition to an overall feedback rating which can be positive, negative or neutral, buyers can leave detailed ratings on four criteria: description accuracy, communication, shipping time, and shipping and handling charges. The ratings, which don't count toward overall feedback scores, range from one to five stars, with five stars being best. The stars are displayed in your feedback profile.

Unlike the overall feedback rating, Detailed Seller Ratings are anonymous.

Keep a good reputation

Maintaining excellent customer service and setting clear expectations in your product descriptions can help keep your feedback record sparkling.

- **Prompt shipping.** Buyers expect prompt shipment and a confirmation of shipment. Part-time sellers can probably get by shipping two or three times per week, but if you take your business seriously, commit yourself to shipping on a daily basis. That way, if you forget a package one day, you're likely to catch your mistake the following day. Aim higher than the minimum requirements.

Justified or not, a substantial portion of buyer feedback comments are gripes about delivery time. "Prompt delivery" and "I received it in a few days" are typical feedback comments from satisfied customers. "Very slow" is an all-too-typical feedback comment, and obviously, the customer could actually be rating the Postal Service rather than the seller.

So it's unavoidable that seller ratings will suffer from slow delivery and other issues outside your control. The best way to minimize problems from delivery speed is shipping as promptly as possible. Daily shipping is not required, but usually results in greater customer satisfaction and less wasted time responding to e-mails from impatient buyers.

Most sellers offer at least two shipping options, express and standard. For example, you can offer Postal Service airmail or ground delivery. Most buyers rarely choose to pay for expedited shipping, but have no qualms about complaining when standard shipping fails to arrive within a week or so.

For sellers of media items such as books, music and videos, the U.S. Postal Service's Media Mail service is usually the most economical shipping option. The drawback with Media Mail (formerly known as Book Rate) is that it can take anywhere from two to four weeks to arrive, resulting in irate customers. More and more, a shipping time exceeding two weeks prompts complaints, especially from younger buyers more accustomed to prompt deliveries by UPS and FedEx.

To minimize grief over tardy Media Mail packages, some sellers upgrade the shipping on lightweight items to First Class or Priority Mail, particularly for customers outside the continental United States. Delivery to Alaska, Hawaii and overseas military and government offices frequently takes longer than 30 days. If you can fit the item into a flat-rate Priority Mail envelope or box, you'll usually save lots of postage compared with paying by weight.

• **Offer unconditional guarantees.** Nothing puts a buyer at ease faster than a strong guarantee. Whether you like it or not, as a seller you're already bound by various requirements from eBay and mail-order requirements that you accept returns from customers. Instead of resisting these requirements, turn them around to work in your favor. Tell your customers that you'll accept returns within 30 days, no questions asked. The vast majority of buyers can't be bothered to return an item even if they decide they don't like it, but a strong guarantee is a confidence-booster for wavering buyers.

While you're thinking about it, compose a detailed payment and shipping policy. Explain how you'll ship and when, when you post feedback, how long you hold checks, and so on. You'll appear more professional, and in case of misunderstanding you'll have your process in writing.

According to research by eBay, buyers' fear of difficulty in returning items is the No. 1 barrier to online sales. Sellers who clearly spell out their policies have a big advantage over competitors and sell a higher percentage of their listings.

To discourage returns, some sellers charge a "restocking fee." For example, a seller who charges a 5 percent restocking fee would refund 95 percent of the customer's purchase price after accepting a return. Also, some sellers refuse to accept "open box" returns, or returns without all the original materials such as the owner's manual. These types of policies should be clearly outlined by the seller to prevent misunderstandings with customers.

Whatever your policies are, be sure to explain them in a friendly way. You don't want to give buyers the impression that you're looking for reasons *not* to do business with them.

● **State your return policy.** To make sure buyers know your return policy, make these notations to the "Additional Information" section of the Sell Your Item form:

- Check the **Returns accepted** check box.

- Pick a time limit for buyers to return items.

- Select the type of refund you'll give if an item is returned— exchange, merchandise credit, or money back. Buyers usually prefer the option of getting their money back.

● Enter additional information about your return policy in the box labeled **Return Policy Details.** For example, will you accept an item for return if the box was opened? If the box is missing? If the item was damaged during return shipping?

● **Offer immediate shipment on personal checks under $25.** If you accept personal checks, consider offering immediate shipment for payments under $25 if a buyer has good feedback. Another option is to hold the merchandise for just a few days after depositing the check. Banks are very efficient these days in clearing check payments.

Completing sales. Prompt, courteous communication and shipping is the bare minimum for succeeding as a seller. If you're using eBay's Checkout feature, the task of contacting your buyer is handled automatically. Otherwise, you'll need to e-mail your buyer to specify the shipping cost, how you'll ship the item to them, a tracking number when available, total price, which payment methods you'll take, and any taxes applied.

EBay will provide you with your buyer's e-mail address in an e-mail notifying you of the end of your listing. You can also contact recent buyers by going through My eBay. Under the heading **All Selling**, click **Sold.** Click on the buyer's nickname, and on the next page you'll see a link for **Contact Member**. Using eBay's messaging system, you can send an e-mail reminding them of the item name and number, bid amount, shipping cost, and payment options.

Another way of spurring a buyer into action is to send a "payment reminder," which you can do after three days and up to 30 days after a transaction. Your buyer receives an e-mail message from eBay with all the pertinent details. To send a payment reminder:

● Go to **My eBay**

● In the left column, click on **Sold.**

- Find the item in question, and click the icon in the item's **Payment Reminder** column.

- Check boxes for each element you want to appear in the e-mail.

- Preview and send the message.

Communicate with a packing slip

You can perform several important functions with a simple packing slip. You can make the customer feel good about the purchase, head off potential problems, and solicit feedback.

Here's sample text you can print on your packing slip to encourage feedback after delivery:

> *Dear Customer:*
>
> *Thank you for your purchase. If you are happy with my service, please leave "feedback" for me, which will let other buyers know I'm a responsible and reliable seller. If you were unsatisfied for any reason, I would appreciate hearing from you before you leave feedback so that I might resolve any issues regarding the transaction.*
>
> *Best regards,*
> *Your Seller*

Notice that the message above provides another opportunity for correcting mistakes and misunderstandings before a customer submits negative feedback.

- **Respond to feedback.** From time to time you may want to publicly respond to a feedback rating or comment you've received. You might want to rebut an inaccurate statement by a buyer or express appreciation to a thankful buyer. Here's how:

- Go to the Reply to Feedback Received page:

http://feedback.ebay.com/ws/eBayISAPI.dll?
PersonalizedFeedbackLogin

- Under the comment where you want to respond, click **Reply.**
Enter your text in the box, and click Leave Reply.

Leave feedback for buyers

You can easily leave feedback ratings for all your transactions from the previous 90 days by visiting My eBay. To leave feedback:

- Click **My eBay** at the top of any eBay page.
- In the left column, click **Feedback** under My Account.
- Click **Leave Feedback.**

Limit your comments to factual statements. Your response can't be deleted, so it's best to avoid writing feedback responses while you're angry. It's better to take a few hours to cool off. Remember, don't take feedback comments personally.

- **Request negative feedback removal.** Protect your feedback average by asking buyers to remove negative ratings you believe are unfair. eBay calls the process "mutual feedback withdrawal," and you can initiate the process by visiting this address:

http://feedback.ebay.com/ws/
eBayISAPI.dll?MFWRequest

A polite request will result in feedback removal about 60 percent of the time. If the buyer cooperates and removes the rating, it will be removed from your feedback page and will no longer be counted toward your average. So it's well worth the effort.

This is where having a script on hand really helps. You're likely to be angry after receiving a negative rating, particularly from an ill-informed buyer. Your first instinct may be to give your customer an earful and try to shame him into removing feedback, but the response will likely be defensiveness and intransigence.

Below is a sample script to request removal of a negative feedback rating in cases where the buyer is unhappy about slow delivery by the Postal Service, even though the seller shipped the item promptly. Notice that it achieves three key objectives:

- Apologizing for the slow delivery.

- Gently explaining that the customer received the promised service.

- Suggesting how the buyer can avoid the problem on future purchases.

> Dear [Buyer]:
>
> I noticed the negative feedback rating you left on my eBay account regarding the delivery time of your item. I apologize that delivery took so long. However, I did ship your package within 24 hours using standard mail, as described on my eBay listing.
>
> I would greatly appreciate it if you would remove the feedback comment. I'm concerned that other buyers may avoid purchasing from me after reading it.
>
> For future reference, you can ensure three-day delivery from me and other eBay sellers by selecting Priority Mail shipping where available.
>
> Best regards,
> Your Seller

If the delay by the Postal Service was egregious, you might offer to sweeten the deal by refunding the shipping fee. Faced with this offer, many buyers respond: "No refund is necessary, I will remove the feedback." You've given the customer a way to save face and claim the moral high ground while cleaning up your feedback.

- **Mutual Feedback Withdrawal.** When your buyer withdraws their feedback, their rating (positive, negative or neutral) disappears from your feedback score. The feedback comment itself remains, but as you continue selling and compile more feedback, the comment text becomes obscured by recent feedback.

You can request Mutual Feedback Withdrawal only once for each rating. You can file your request within 30 days of the feedback left by you or your transaction partner, or 90 days after the transaction date, whichever is later.

- **Feedback Removal.** A last resort for getting inappropriate feedback removed is requesting feedback removal by eBay, which is a long shot. The company will completely erase the feedback and all comments, but only if it violates its Feedback Removal and Abuse Policy.

To qualify for removal by eBay, feedback must meet one or more of these circumstances:

- eBay receives a valid court order showing the feedback in question is "slanderous, libelous, defamatory or illegal."

- Comments in the feedback include language judged "profane, vulgar, obscene, or racist" or of an "adult" nature. Inflammatory language describing a transaction partner as a "fraud, liar, cheater, scam artist, con man," etc., is strongly discouraged by eBay, but doesn't necessarily qualify for removal.

- The comments in the feedback include personal identifying data such as another member's real name, address, phone number, or e-mail.

- The feedback refers to an investigation by police, eBay or Pay-Pal.

- The feedback contains HTML links or scripts.

- Feedback was left by a buyer who wasn't eligible to participate in eBay transactions according to Section 1 of eBay's user agreement.

- Feedback was from a buyer who gave eBay false contact information and therefore couldn't be contacted during the "transaction period" 30 days after the feedback posting date or 90 days from the end of the listing, whichever is longer.

- Feedback was from a buyer who eBay determines bid on or bought an item solely in order to leave negative feedback, and didn't intend to complete the transaction.

- Feedback from buyers who are indefinitely suspended for violating certain eBay policies within 90 days of registration.

Sometimes a buyer makes a mistake and leaves negative feedback for the wrong seller. It's possible to get this feedback removed by eBay, but only when the buyer notifies eBay of the mistake and posts the same feedback for the correct seller. For more details, see:

http://pages.ebay.com/help/policies/feedback-abuse-withdrawal.html

- **SquareTrade.com.** SquareTrade, a company that provides dispute resolution services, is another option for resolving feedback problems. SquareTrade uses a panel of professional mediators who help sellers resolve disputes with buyers for a fee of $29.95. Membership is $9.50 per month or $95 per year with prepayment. However, with the introduction of eBay's free Mutual Feedback Withdrawal procedure a few years ago, it seems that SquareTrade is less popular with sellers than it used to be.

- **Feedback policies.** Any discussion of eBay's feedback policies would be incomplete without mentioning the following prohibitions. Violations of these guidelines can result in restriction or suspension of a member's account:

  - **Feedback Extortion.** Threatening negative or neutral feedback for a seller unless the seller provides a good or service not included in the original listing.

  - **Feedback Manipulation.** Feedback whose primary purpose is to "artificially" enhance an eBayer's reputation.

  - **Feedback in Seller Terms and Conditions.** Sellers are prohibited from restricting the buyer from leaving feedback.

Appropriate time for feedback. Some sellers make it a habit of leaving feedback for their buyers as soon as they receive payment. Their theory is that upon payment, the buyer has fulfilled his end of the bargain. And eBay's research shows that sellers who leave feedback immediately tend to receive more feedback from buyers.

On the other hand, many sellers avoid leaving feedback until they have received a positive rating from the buyer. Their philosophy is that nothing prevents buyers from leaving inappropriate feedback once the seller has already left the buyer a positive rating.

One valid reason for waiting until a buyer leaves feedback is this can be taken as a sign a buyer is satisfied, and needs no further customer support.

Feedback stars. After receiving 10 feedback points, eBay members receive stars displayed next to their User ID. The display changes with each successive level of feedback:

Yellow star = 10 to 49 points

Blue star = 50 to 99 points

Turquoise star = 100 to 499 points

Purple star = 500 to 999 points

Red star = 1,000 to 4,999 points

Green star = 5,000 to 9,999 points

Yellow shooting star = 10,000 to 24,999 points

Turquoise shooting star = 25,000 to 49,999 points

Purple shooting star = 50,000 to 99,999 points

Red shooting star = 100,000 points or more

Handle customers right

You need cooperation from buyers on removing inappropriate feedback because eBay will rarely get involved in a dispute. In general, the company's policy is to remove feedback only when the feedback contains obscene language or it includes personal information such as your full name or telephone number.

Unfortunately, some buyers are just impossible to satisfy. Perhaps the buyer doesn't understand the feedback process, won't admit a mistake, or is just plain malicious. When all attempts to make amends fail, the important thing is to avoid taking it personally. Learn what you can from the experience and move on. Don't let a dispute with an unreasonable buyer distract you from running your business.

Unpaid item disputes

eBay buyers are legally bound to purchase your item if they win the auction or use Buy It Now. If a buyer receives excessive unpaid items "strikes," their account can be suspended. Regardless, you will occasionally have buyers who neglect to pay and don't respond when you attempt to contact them. Your alternative is to begin a four-step unpaid item process:

● **File Dispute.** You can report an unpaid item as long as 45 days after the transaction date. Usually you're required to wait seven days to file the dispute, but you can file immediately if the buyer is no longer registered at eBay or both parties agree to cancel the transaction. Visit this URL to report your dispute:

http://rebulk.ebay.com/ws/eBayISAPI.dll?CreateDispute

- **eBay contacts your buyer.** Via e-mail and pop-up message, eBay reminds your buyer to pay and provides instructions. If the buyer fails to respond within seven days, you can file for a Final Value Fee credit and you'll be eligible for a relist fee credit.

- **Mutual agreement indication.** If you indicate that you've reached an agreement with your buyer to not complete the transaction, eBay will ask for confirmation from your buyer through an e-mail and pop-up message. If the buyer confirms your statement about mutually agreeing to not complete the transaction, you'll receive the Final Value Fee credit. If your buyer disagrees with your statement on mutual agreement, you won't receive a Final Value Fee credit and the dispute will be closed. If the buyer doesn't respond within seven days, you'll be able to close the dispute, and you'll receive a Final Value Fee credit.

- **Item Dispute Communication.** Your buyer has three options. They can elect to pay immediately with PayPal or with another payment method. Your buyer's other options are indicating they've already paid, or they'll communicate with you about paying.

- **Closing the dispute.** From your Dispute Console, you can close disputes when the buyer has responded or if the buyer fails to respond within eight days. You have three options for closing disputes:
  1. **We've completed the transaction and we're both satisfied.** You won't receive the Final Value Fee credit, and your buyer doesn't receive an Unpaid Item strike.
  2. **We've agreed not to complete the transaction.** You'll receive a Final Value Fee credit and be eligible for a relist credit, and your buyer won't receive an Unpaid Item strike.
  3. **I no longer wish to communicate with or wait for the buyer.** You'll receive a Final Value Fee credit and be eligible

for a relist credit, and your buyer will receive an Unpaid Item strike.

If the dispute isn't closed within 60 days of the transaction, eBay closes it automatically. In this case you won't receive a Final Value Fee credit, and your buyer won't receive an Unpaid Item strike. Buyers and sellers are able to leave feedback on transactions connected with an Unpaid Item dispute, even after reaching a mutual agreement not to complete the transaction.

Prevent unpaid items

Follow these four steps to reduce your rate of unpaid items:

- Accept PayPal, which makes it easier for buyers to pay.

- Provide clear shipping and handling information in your listing's description and "shipping details" section. If this section is vague or blank, most buyers will move on, and you'll lose the sale.

- Use eBay Checkout, which makes it simple for buyers to pay.

- For fixed-price listings, require immediate payment through PayPal.

Work with PayPal

PayPal is a fast, easy way to collect payments securely over the Internet. When you accept PayPal, your eBay buyers can pay you with a credit card or checking account without having to send you their account number or any personal information. PayPal is owned by eBay, and you can use it for your eBay transactions or on your own Web site.

Most sellers see two big advantages of using PayPal:

- You get paid faster. You don't have to wait for a check or money order to arrive in the mail.

- Many buyers prefer PayPal because it's easy and quick. So offering PayPal on your listings will usually result in more sales for you.

The disadvantage to PayPal is that sellers incur an extra fee on each transaction. However, many sellers believe that PayPal brings in extra business that offsets the fees. And unlike many other merchant credit card systems, PayPal requires no setup fees, no membership fees, and no minimum transaction requirements.

If you don't already have a PayPal account, it's simple enough to get started. Simply select PayPal as a payment method on the Sell Your Item form and enter the e-mail address where you want to be notified of payments. When you get your first payment you'll be asked to sign up.

You can also use PayPal to accept payments from overseas customers if you upgrade your account to a Premier or Business account. You can accept payments from customers in 50 countries, and the foreign currencies are automatically converted into U.S. dollars for you.

PayPal provides protection programs for buyers and sellers. The **Seller Protection Policy** protects sellers from complaints and chargebacks if certain conditions are met, such as proof of delivery through a parcel tracking system.

PayPal's **Buyer Protection Policy** allows customers to file a complaint within 45 days if they don't receive an item or the item is significantly different than the seller's description. Also, if the buyer used a credit card to fund the PayPal transaction, they can initiate a chargeback through their credit card company to obtain a refund.

Sellers who receive an "item not received" claim from PayPal are asked to enter a tracking number for the parcel on the company's Web site. If the buyer claims that an item is "significantly not as described," PayPal usually requires the buyer to return the item to the seller at the buyer's expense, with proof of return delivery.

PayPal security keys. In 2007, PayPal introduced an optional security key, adding another layer of protection for users logging into PayPal or eBay. Users press a button on the key, then enter a six-digit code to complete their login. PayPal charges $5 for the device.

Refunding buyers. If you decide to refund a buyer for a transaction, you'll normally use the same payment method as the buyer used. To issue a refund with PayPal:

- At **www.paypal.com**, log into your account.

- On the **My Account Overview** page, find the item you need to refund, and then click **Details**.

- If you don't see the item that needs a refund, click on the **All Activity** link.

- On the **Transaction Details** page, click **Refund Payment** near the bottom of the item page. Follow the directions to issue the refund.

Set your payment preferences

You can change your payment preferences on eBay by clicking **Preferences** in My eBay under "My Account." Click **Show** in the "Payment from buyers" section.

You can edit any of these settings:

- **Use Checkout.** When Checkout is on, your buyer sees **Pay Now** buttons when purchasing from you. If Checkout is off, you'll need to send your buyer an invoice in order to use Checkout. The default setting is on.

- **PayPal Preferred.** Your buyers are notified on the item page that you prefer PayPal. The default setting is off.

- **Buyer Edit Payment Totals Option.** When this setting is on, your buyer is able to edit the payment amount during Checkout. For example, the buyer would be able to add additional fees for overnight delivery or gift wrapping. Default setting is on.

- **Payment Address.** Your payment address is displayed only when a buyer wants to pay with a check or other method that requires sending postal mail to your physical address.

- **Multiple Seller Payments.** Enables buyers to pay for multiple items from different sellers simultaneously with one payment. Each seller receives a separate payment from PayPal.

"Verifying" your PayPal account enables you to raise your withdrawal and sending limits. If you already have an account, you can become PayPal-Verified by logging in, clicking the **PayPal Verified** icon, and following the instructions. If you don't have an account yet, you can become Verified as part of the signup process.

If you commit to selling full-time, you should upgrade your PayPal account to a Business account. You'll be able to conduct your transactions in your business name. To upgrade your account, click on the **Sign Up** link at PayPal's home page.

Take payments

Payments policy. You have many options for accepting payments on eBay, and each has its advantages and disadvantages. Some of the most popular payment methods:

- **PayPal.** As stated previously, eBay strongly encourages the use of PayPal, and eBay owns the company. Sellers who have a different merchant credit card account or a third-party processor can offer this option to buyers, either through a third-party checkout process or by telephone.

- **Money orders and cashier's checks.** In theory, this is one of the safest payment methods for sellers, but the frequency of check forgeries in recent years has reduced the attractiveness. On the other hand, the odds that you'll receive a phony money order or cashier's check from a eBay buyer who has a good feedback record are exceedingly small.

- **Personal checks.** This is a popular payment method with many buyers. But checks create extra work for sellers, who must fill out deposit slips to deposit the checks at their banks. Also, you've got to wait for the buyer to send the check in the mail. And, even with small payment amounts, there is always the chance that the check will bounce.

Other payment methods permitted on eBay: PayPal, credit cards including MasterCard, Visa, American Express, Discover, debit cards and bank electronic payments. Sellers can also accept bank wire transfers or bank cash transfers. Cash on delivery (COD) or cash for in-person transactions are allowed. Sellers may accept personal checks, cashier's checks, money orders and certified checks.

Here are examples of payment methods permitted on eBay: All-pay.net, cash2india, CertaPay, CheckFree, hyperwallet.com, Moneybookers.com, Nochex.com, Ozpay.biz, Paymate.com.au, Propay.com, and XOOM.

Not permitted on eBay: Sellers aren't allowed to ask buyers to send cash through the mail. Likewise, sellers are prohibited from asking buyers to pay using instant cash transfer services such as Western Union or Moneygram.

eBay doesn't allow the use of Google Checkout or these other payment methods: AlertPay.com, anypay.com, AuctionChex.com, BillPay.ie, ecount.com, cardserviceinternational.com, CCAvenue, ecount, e-gold, eHotPay.com, ePassporte.com, EuroGiro, Fast-Cash.com, gcash, GearPay, Goldmoney.com, graphcard.com, greenzap.com, ikobo.com, Liberty Dollars, Moneygram.com, ne-teller.com, Netpay.com, paychest.com, payingfast.com, Payko.com, paypay, Postepay, Qchex.com, rupay.com, sendmoneyorder.com, stamps, Stormpay, wmtransfer.com, xcoin.com.

PayPal and credit cards. If you choose to accept PayPal during the listing process, you're obligated to accept all forms of PayPal payments, including credit cards, bank accounts and PayPal balances. Sellers who assert they will not accept PayPal credit card payments are in violation of eBay and PayPal rules.

Your seller account. Each month eBay will send you an invoice for all your applicable Insertion Fees, Final Value Fees, and additional fees for optional features. Non-payment of your seller fees can lead to account suspension. You can view or download recent account activity through My eBay.

You'll have several options for paying your seller fees, including PayPal, credit card, direct payments, by check (business checks, not personal checks). You may pay after receiving your invoice, or you can sign up for automatic monthly payments.

Fees. There's no membership fee for selling on eBay. Your cost for selling items is the combination of your **Insertion Fees** and **Final Value Fees.** When creating an eBay listing, you'll be able to view an itemized list of all fees before submitting your listing. For a listing of current eBay fee, see:

http://pages.ebay.com/help/sell/fees.html

When you list an item for sale on eBay, you're charged a non-refundable **Insertion Fee.** The higher your starting price or Reserve Price is, the higher your Insertion Fee will be. Insertion Fees for a Multiple Item Auction (Dutch Auction) and Fixed Price listings depend on the opening value of your items. The opening value is the starting price or fixed price multiplied by the quantity listed.

When you sell an item you'll pay the **Final Value** Fee, a set percentage plus some additional fees if your item sells for more than $25.

Optional Feature Fees. You can increase your odds of a successful sale by adding optional features, but you'll incur additional fees for doing so.

Reserve Fees are $1 for reserve prices under $50 and $2 for reserve prices from $50 to $199.99. For a reserve price of $200 and up, you'll pay 1 percent of the Reserve Price (up to $50). If your item sells, your Reserve Fees will be refunded.

When you sell an item from a fixed-price listing, you'll pay a **Buy It Now Fee.** The greater your price, the larger the fee.

eBay offers several listing upgrades for optional features such as subtitles, bold titles, and gallery pictures. Many of these optional features can be bundled together into special packages. eBay also charges some fees for additional picture hosting beyond what's included in a basic insertion fee.

Use Skype. Skype is an online conferencing system owned by eBay that allows users to talk to other users for free and eliminate long-distance phone charges. You download software to your computer and set up a microphone and earpiece.

Sellers can add Skype buttons to their listings, allowing buyers to contact them and ask questions. You can add voice or chat capability to your listings, which helps build confidence with buyers of complicated or expensive items. See:

http://pages.ebay.com/skype/

Avoid scams and fraud

The good news about eBay is it's a vibrant marketplace and a great place to do business. The bad news is, every lively bazaar attracts its share of crooks, and if you're careless you'll be victimized.

Use care in choosing your eBay User ID, password and "secret question." Your User ID is the seller nickname that identifies you on eBay. Select a name and password unrelated to your e-mail address and other online accounts. Using similar log-in information at different sites is risky—if one account is compromised, the rest of your accounts will be at risk. Also, a unique User ID helps you avoid spam.

A good, secure password includes a combination of at least six to eight letters, numbers and special characters. It's also a good idea to change your eBay password every couple of months.

In the event you ever forget your password, go to eBay's "Forgot Your Password" page:

**http://cgi4.ebay.com/ws/
eBayISAPI.dll?ForgotYourPasswordShow**

You'll need to enter your User ID and verify your identity. eBay then will e-mail instructions for resetting your password.

If you forget your User ID, visit the Forgot User ID page:

**http://cgi4.ebay.com/
ws/eBayISAPI.dll?UserIdRecognizerShow**

You can change your password by visiting eBay's "Change Your Password" page:

**http://signin.ebay.com/
ws/eBayISAPI.dll?ChangePasswordAndCreateHint**

Spot shady buyers

Counterfeit cashier's checks are an increasingly popular technique for scammers. Crooks are easily able to use software and laser printers to create phony checks. Here are typical warning signs:

• You're selling a high-priced item and receive a request from a foreign bidder to accept a foreign cashier's check.

• The amount of a cashier's check you receive is much more than the value of the item. The buyer wants you to overnight the excess payment using a cash wire transfer service such as Western Union or Money-gram.

Experience shows this scenario is dangerous. It may take many weeks for your bank to discover the check was fake. If the cashier's check is fraudulent, you'll be required to reimburse your bank.

Another technique popular with scammers is pressuring eBayers to avoid using PayPal or checks in favor of Western Union and other cash-transfer services where the payment can't be canceled or reversed. For more information on auction fraud and how to report it, consult the AuctionBytes fraud resource:

http://www.auctionbytes.com/cab/pages/fraud

Recognize predators

Avoid phishing e-mails. Crooks on the Internet will try to steal your eBay account and password by sending phony e-mails that appear to be from eBay itself. Typically, the e-mail will warn that your account will be suspended or canceled unless you log into a Web site (supposedly eBay's) and provide your account information.

It's highly unlikely eBay would send a message asking about your account number, password, or other personal information, but if it did, you'd receive a copy in your **My Messages** box at My eBay. Otherwise, that suspicious e-mail is a phishing attempt.

If you're not certain a message is really from eBay, don't click on links contained in the e-mail. Instead, open a new browser window, go to ebay.com, and sign in. If the message doesn't appear in My Messages, it's a phish, often called a "spoof" message.

Spoof messages usually have an official-looking eBay logo and may appear to have an eBay address in the "From" line, such as "help@ebay.com."

Typically, spoof e-mails have one or more of the following characteristics:

- Requests personal information, such as "Please update your credit card number."

- Doesn't address you by name, but a generic phrase such as "Dear eBay member."

- Demands immediate action, such as "Failure to respond will result in suspension of your account within two business days."

- Links to Web pages that mimic eBay's real sign-in page. An example of a spoof link is http://signin-ebay.com.

If you receive a suspicious e-mail, report it to eBay by forwarding the message to spoof@ebay.com. eBay will check the message and notify you if it was really sent by eBay.

eBay offers a free "Account Guard" toolbar you can download and install to your Web browser. The toolbar indicates when you are on a verified eBay or PayPal Web site and warns you when you're visiting a potential spoof site. The toolbar, which also helps protect your eBay password, is available here:

http://pages.ebay.com/ebay_toolbar

Using My Messages. As discussed previously, eBay's **My Messages** is a secure area where you receive messages from eBay as well as other eBay members. Here you'll typically receive messages from buyers who used eBay's **Ask a Question** feature. When you respond to the message, eBay will send a copy to your customer's My Messages inbox and to their registered e-mail address. A copy will also be saved in your My Messages **Sent** folder and (if you check the required box) to your registered e-mail address.

For more information, see eBay's tutorial on spoof e-mails:

http://pages.ebay.com/education/spooftutorial/

Beware of hoax e-mails

By Ina Steiner, AuctionBytes.com

Every year, thousands of unsuspecting eBay sellers have their accounts hijacked by scammers who send hoax e-mails. The messages, disguised to look as though they are coming from eBay and PayPal, trick eBay members into revealing their password, banking and credit card information.

The perpetrators, often called "phishers," attempt to lure recipients into clicking on a link embedded in the e-mail directing them to a "spoof" log-in page, set up to look just like eBay or PayPal. The user unwittingly logs into the fake site with their user name and password and enters private information that is harvested by the scammers.

Some hoax e-mails are easy to spot because bad grammar gives them away. An example:

Dear PayPal user!
At 09.27.2003 our company has lost a number of accounts in the system during the database maintenance.

Or this one:

Subj: Your acount will be dezactivated
From: suspension@eBay.com (suspension@eBay.com)
Reply-to: suspension@eBay.com (suspension@eBay.com)

Although you can get a good chuckle out of the more inept attempts to gain your personal information, some scam e-mails are very sophisticated, and extremely difficult to distinguish from the "real" notifications.

Sometimes the message sounds plausible, such as asking a user to update their eBay account information because of a security breach. Many times they use a sense of urgency to get you to respond right away, before you have time to think about it being a possible scam.

We had a security breach, we will shut down your account if you don't immediately verify your account information, click on the link below.
We regret to inform you that your eBay account will be suspended if you don't resolve your problems.

Here's one that's quite convincing:

We regret to inform you that your eBay account has been suspended due to concerns we have for the safety and integrity of the eBay community.

Per the User Agreement, Section 9, we may immediately issue a warning, temporarily suspend, indefinitely suspend or terminate your membership and refuse to provide our services to you if we believe that your actions may cause financial loss or legal liability for you, our users or us. We may also take these actions if we are unable to verify or authenticate any information you provide to us.

Please note that any seller fees due to eBay will immediately become due and payable. eBay will charge any amounts you have not previously disputed to the billing method currently on file.

To activate your suspended eBay account please complete the
form located at...

Be safe. Never click on a link in an e-mail to log in to an account. Always go to your Web browser, type in the URL of the site, and log in as you normally would. Don't think that just because you've been on the Internet for a long time that you are immune—some very smart people have been tricked into giving out personal credit information as a result of these hoax e-mails!

Steiner is co-founder and editor of AuctionBytes, an independent source of news, tips, and opinions for the eBay community. For more information on marketing, product sourcing, and product reviews, see AuctionBytes.com.

Avoid drop-ship, wholesale scams

Drop-shipping is a popular topic of discussion among eBay sellers who are trying to expand their businesses. With drop-shipping, you offer to sell merchandise that someone else has on hand. When you get a sale, the other party "drop-ships" it for you.

On the Internet, you'll probably discover many companies offering to drop-ship products to your eBay buyers. It sounds great because they promise you big profits, while they handle the shipping. But just remember the familiar saying, "If it sounds too good to be true..."

Think about it: If it was so easy to sell the merchandise from this drop-shipping company at huge profits, then the drop-shipping company would probably be busy selling it themselves, and they wouldn't be inviting you to compete with them.

Many of the drop-shipping offers out there are simply scams. In other cases, the companies are legitimate, but it's just impossible to earn money by working with them. When several eBay sellers are selling the same merchandise, price competition results in slim profits for everyone.

One way that sellers can drop-ship successfully is by working directly with a manufacturer or a master distributor. This ensures there is no middleman, and there will still be enough of a profit margin for you. But this isn't easy. Many manufacturers and distributors don't actively look for small businesses to sell their merchandise on the Web. Many companies simply don't want their goods available on eBay or anywhere else online because it angers traditional retailers who don't want the competition.

You'll find directories of wholesalers, importers, and drop-shippers for sale on eBay, but these often contain outdated, inaccurate or useless information. Instead, consult a real directory such as *American Wholesalers And Distributors Directory* at your public library. You may also be able to find a directory of product manufacturers for your state, or an export-import trade business directory. Also, the reference librarian may be able to point you toward online directories that you'd have to pay a hefty subscription fee for if you were using your home computer.

If you contact a manufacturer, they'll nearly always say they don't deal directly with retailers. Use the opportunity to ask them for a recommendation for a wholesaler for their products.

And remember, legitimate wholesalers and manufacturers won't deal with you unless you're operating a legal business. We'll discuss this in a subsequent section, but at a minimum, this means:

- You've filed a business name with your county or state government. Usually this is done by filing a fictitious name or DBA (doing business as) application with your county government, or by incorporating your business by filing paperwork with your state government.

- You have a Tax ID authorizing you to collect sales tax on sales made to customers within your state. In some cases this is called a "seller's permit" or "use tax certificate."

- A business bank account. You'll need your business name paperwork to open a business (not personal) bank account.

Recognize crooks and middlemen

In the book *What to Sell on eBay and Where to Get It*, authors Chris Malta and Lisa Suttora explain that most of the advertisements you'll come across for wholesalers and drop-shipping companies are actually middlemen or multilevel marketing schemes. Either one will produce headaches for your business. Here are the authors' tips on recognizing the scammers:

Warning signs of bogus wholesalers:

- Does not include a full company name, address, and phone number that they answer.

- Makes claims about how much money you can make by doing business with them.

- The "wholesaler" is offering the same products you can find on other "wholesale" Web sites.

- The site attempts to sell other services or membership fees in addition to offering wholesale products.

- The wholesaler does not ask for your Sales Tax ID before accepting an order.

If you have any doubt about whether a wholesaler is legitimate, investigating is a straightforward matter:

- Search the Internet for the company's name. If other online sellers have had problems with the company, you'll find complaints quickly.

- Search for complaints about the company at the Better Business Bureau, www.BBB.org.

- Contact the Chamber of Commerce in the city where the company operates. Even if the company is not a chamber member, the group should have some information about them.

Know a fake from the real McCoy

By Ken Zajac

Increased interest and prices in many collectible categories have been a boon for eBay sellers. But along with the high prices comes a big downside: the emergence of authentic-looking fakes.

In the 1980s and 1990s Art Pottery hit a peak in sales and prices, with many pieces selling for far above reference book prices. This high market caused such an interest that another market developed—the production of **fake** pottery, and **reproduction** or **repro** pottery. There is a difference between the two.

The marketing of fakes and reproductions devalues the originals, causing an atmosphere of suspicion among collectors and investors. The best defense against this corruption in the marketplace is education.

Fakes are pieces that were made to deceive. Fakes have shapes and patterns that look similar to an original, or have characteristics of pieces an original manufacturer might have made, but didn't.

Reproductions are pieces that usually have been made from the original molds, but they were made recently, and not by the companies that made the molds. This can happen when the molds have been sold after the original company closed, usually some decades later.

Fake pottery offered for sale is quite often made in China, but isn't marked that way. The China fakers attempt to mark the original manufacturer's name on the pieces. But a quick comparison between the China marks and the original marks reveals the difference. There isn't the same attention to detail, and the color of the clay used to make the pieces sometimes shows through around the mark on the bottom.

New fakes are usually made with light or white-color clay. The bottom rim and, sometimes, the inside typically has no glaze, and appears clean. The craftsmanship on fakes is poor. They have vague patterns, rough features, bright glazing colors, and generally lack the hand-worked quality of originals.

Reproduction pottery is more difficult to assess. Original pottery companies usually kept their molds, even after they closed their businesses. The molds were sold, and the new owners of the molds started new production using the original molds. Another repro method is to make a new mold from an original piece. The big difference is that the clay used in repros is not the same as the original clays. Repros made from an original piece rather than an old mold will always be of slightly smaller size than the original piece. Also, the glazing is new. Sometimes the glaze will not entirely cover the piece, and you can see bright clay where the glazing missed. Sometimes the bottom rim will not be glazed, revealing that it's a repro. And the bright glazing colors can give away the age, although old and original pieces in mint condition will look bright too.

The fakers have gotten good at their deceptions, they sometimes make the bottom rims with artificial wear and dirty-looking unglazed clay. Some have defects introduced deliberately, mimicking old damage. Many of the patents from the original companies have been granted to subsidiary companies that make fakes, which allows them to legally make and sell fakes.

When looking at online auctions for purchasing pottery, if you are not sure about the piece you want, try searching the Internet for the same manufacturer. Chances are you will find a number of Web sites that show photos of originals and fakes. Fakes are plentiful, and most reliable groups will show you what the differences are.

Some reliable sources of information are the American Art Pottery Association, Wisconsin Pottery Association, and the Glass & Pottery Seller's Association, among others.

Zajac is an antiques dealer in Tacoma, Wash.

Pack it up, move it out

So far, we've seen how important it is to keep up with customer communications on a daily basis. That is the mental part of the selling process. Now we'll examine the physical aspect of fulfilling orders.

Devising a routine way of storing, retrieving, and packing items for shipping can help you save a bit of time with each transaction, leading to a huge cumulative impact in time savings. And as we know, time is money.

Standardizing the way you handle customer orders will minimize mistakes and help you operate faster and more efficiently. Likewise, striving to obtain the best rates on postage and delivery confirmation has a huge cumulative effect on your profitability.

Ship efficiently

Determine which type of shipping materials you'll need to ship all your merchandise, and be sure to keep adequate packing supplies on hand. The less time you spend each day scrounging around for the proper packing materials, the more time you'll have for finding and listing new merchandise.

Three popular choices for packaging are cardboard boxes, corrugated boxes and bubble mailers. The type and value of the item being shipped can call for different materials. Padded or bubble envelopes may be fine for small, inexpensive items, but for more fragile and valuable items, use a box to protect from bending and crushing.

Local stores like Staples and Office Depot have decent prices on shipping supplies, but you can find a wider selection and save money by buying shipping supplies online in quantity through vendors like Associated Bag Co. and Uline. There are many perfectly fine sellers of packing materials right on eBay. If you can get a cost savings of 20 cents for each bubble mailer, for example, that adds up to a fair amount of money over the year, which you can add to your bottom line.

If you've reached the point where you're shipping more than two packages a day, it's time to consider using an online postage service. Monthly service fees are $15 or less, allowing you to avoid standing in line at the Post Office. Instead, you'll be able to prepare your shipments at your PC and drop off crates of parcels at your Post Office's rear dock. You also can submit a request for "Carrier Pickup," and a Postal Service truck driver will pick up your packages at your house for no charge. For more information, see:

**http://pages.ebay.com
/usps/shippingitems/carrierpickup.html**

Thermal label printers. Another big time-saver is a thermal label printer, which quickly prints 4 x 6-inch address labels like the ones used on UPS packages. Instead of constantly having to feed sheets of labels into a laser printer, you can load a dedicated thermal printer with a roll of 300 labels and it's always ready. Although these printers can cost more than $300 when brand new, used and reconditioned thermal printers are usually available on eBay for about $40.

Likewise, a postal scale with at least a 10-pound capacity can be a valuable time-saver. Don't risk your shipments by using a bathroom scale to weigh your packages. You don't want to apply too little or too much postage. Some of the newer electronic scales integrate with online postage services, saving you even more time because you don't need to key in the package's weight.

Choose a shipping company. An expanding lineup of companies competes for the business of the eBay seller:

- **U.S. Postal Service.** If you're selling typical merchandise, the good old Post Office should be your first consideration. Although USPS takes a fair amount of criticism, its service is relatively reliable and economical. For items weighing less than a few pounds, USPS is usually the cheapest way to ship. The Postal Service also provides free shipping envelopes and boxes for users of its Priority Mail and Express Mail services. Special low rates for sellers of media such as books and videos make the Postal Service indispensable. Although USPS offers delivery confirmation with online tracking numbers, the system is not as reliable as those offered by competitors. For more information, see www.usps.gov.

- **United Parcel Service.** UPS is a good option for packages that are larger and heavier than the maximum accepted by the Postal Service. UPS accepts packages weighing up to 150 pounds, while the USPS maximum is 70 pounds. Nowadays many office supply stores such as Staples have UPS drop-off counters. For more information, see www.ups.com.

- **Federal Express.** FedEx made its name by offering overnight delivery for urgent packages. Since then the company has expanded into Ground Home Delivery service that is fairly economical and comparable to regular UPS service. For more information, see www.fedex.com.

Using eBay's Calculated Shipping Costs. Shipping and handling fees are one of the leading causes of friction between buyers and sellers. Buyers are much more likely to bid and buy if they know they will pay reasonable shipping costs and if they know what the seller's actual shipping costs are.

- Buyers are more forgiving about shipping costs when the fees are transparent. An easy way to show your buyer the actual costs is to use eBay's "Calculated Shipping Costs" feature, which shows shipping and insurance rates from the Postal Service and UPS based on the item's weight and the buyer's ZIP Code. You can add a "handling" cost to cover your costs for packing materials. The total appears on your item page, and is automatically charged to buyers when they pay. You can initiate this feature through the Sell Your Item form. You can also offer "flat" shipping costs. In this case, you set one fee and describe what services you use, such as the Postal Service and UPS.

Printing shipping labels from eBay or PayPal. You can automatically print shipping labels from My eBay or PayPal. To use My eBay:

- Go to **Items I've Sold** and check the box next to each item you're shipping.
- Click **Print Shipping Labels**.
- Log in at PayPal.
- Choose the desired shipping carrier and service.
- Enter package weight, verify the addresses, and click **Print**.

To print labels using PayPal:

- Visit your **Account Overview** page or Post-Sale Manager and click **Ship** for an item.
- Select a carrier and service.
- Enter package weight, verify addresses, and click **Print.**

Tracking packages from My eBay:

- Go to **Items I've sold** and click **View Shipment Status** for an item.
- Click the link under **Shipping Status.**

Communicate when you ship

• **Send a shipment confirmation.** Send your buyers a message confirming the shipment, including a tracking number if you have one. A short message confirming that the item is on the way reassures the customer and prevents unnecessary and time-consuming inquiries days later. One easy way to do this is by replying to payment e-mails from PayPal. Your reply automatically goes to the buyer's PayPal-registered e-mail address.

• **Enclose your contact information.** A packing slip with the order number and your e-mail address will be useful in case you made a mistake filling the order or the customer receives something unexpected. Third-party software tools can automate this procedure, eliminating the need for cutting and pasting. For more information, see appendix 3.

• **Solicit feedback after delivery.** Encourage customers to give you a feedback rating, explaining that it will help you show other potential buyers that you're a trustworthy and reliable seller. Solicit feedback on the packing slip, not in your shipment confirmation e-mail. An early prompting in the shipping confirmation will make some customers impatient, and they might submit a negative rating before their package is due to arrive. The customer is in a better frame of mind after he receives the merchandise.

Pare shipping costs to the bone

By David Steiner, AuctionBytes.com

U.S. Postal Service Priority Mail is a popular shipping method for eBay sellers because of the 2-3 day shipping time, competitive rates and most importantly, free shipping boxes. You can even have the Postal Service deliver the boxes free by ordering online:

http://ebaysupplies.usps.com/

These packages handle most small items, but sometimes it's like trying to squeeze an elephant into a phone booth. With a little ingenuity, there are ways to combine Priority Mail Boxes to cover a wide variety of shapes and sizes. Here are a few suggestions and examples:

• The Empire State Building

Great for long items that don't have much girth. Take a few #4 Priority Mail boxes and slide them together. Tape around the girth of the box and up the sides. This will give you a package that can accommodate an item the shape of a baseball bat, golf club or any long, slender item. Make sure you pad around the item with Styrofoam peanuts so that the item is immobilized in the center. Be aware that items packed like this may be charged a balloon rate by the USPS. That is an extra charge applied when the combined length and girth of a package falls between 84" and 108" and the weight is less than 15 lbs.

• The Sears Tower

Same construction as the Empire State Building, but created with #7 Priority boxes. This allows for shipping items that happen to be taller than a single #7 Priority box. Again, slide the boxes together and tape all seams so that the boxes are firmly bound together.

• The Bonneville Salt Flats

Great for shipping wide and long items that are flat, like a tennis racket. Take two 0-1097 boxes (11-1/4" x 14" x 2-1/4") and slide them together like the two previous examples. Tape them together securely to maintain the package's structural integrity.

There are limitations on what you can do with Priority Mail boxes. You can't turn the boxes inside out and use them for other methods of shipping. Priority Mail boxes are stamped with special codes on the interior cardboard. If, for example, you try to mail book-rate package using a Priority package, you will be charged the Priority rate or be asked to repackage your items. You shouldn't cut up Priority Mail Boxes and use them as padding or to make compartments inside your package.

Now for the packing itself: Use Styrofoam peanuts, not newspaper. Styrofoam peanuts may be more expensive, but they immobilize an item much better than paper and they don't leave newsprint marks. Here's my usual technique:

- Wrap the item in bubble wrap. If the item is silver or some material that might have a reaction to the bubble wrap, I wrap it in paper first, then put the bubble wrap over the paper.

- Add a healthy layer of Styrofoam peanuts to the bottom of the box.

- Place the item in the box on top of the peanuts, making sure there is plenty of empty space on all sides of the item.

- Pour on the peanuts. Don't skimp on this step. Make sure there is plenty of padding around the entire item and pack the peanuts in firmly. The goal is to keep the item immobilized in the center of the box and as far away from the cardboard as possible.

- Add more peanuts to the top of the item. No part of the item should be touching the inside of the box!

The peanuts will give the box more interior strength to help it stand up to other mail being stacked on top of it. If you don't put enough padding in the package, your item will settle or shift, and it will find its way to the bottom of the box, where it is more likely to be damaged.

Steiner is president of Steiner Associates LLC, publisher of AuctionBytes, an independent source of news, tips, and opinions for the eBay community. For more information on marketing, product sourcing, and product reviews, see AuctionBytes.com.

Sell Get It Fast Items

eBay's Get It Fast program promises buyers that a purchased item will arrive promptly. The program reassures buyers who are looking for holiday and gift items, so participating can increase your sales during those periods.

To participate, select the **Get it Fast** check box in the Sell Your Item form's shipping section when you list items. In doing so, you commit to the following:

- Shipping within one business day of receiving cleared payment. On the Sell Your Item form, select **1 business day** from the menu for "Domestic handling time."

- Offering a domestic overnight shipping service such as FedEx, UPS Next Day Air or Postal Service Express Mail.

Remember that you're committing to a one-day response time, even if your customer doesn't upgrade to overnight delivery.

Handle delivery snafus

Sometimes a Postal Service carrier scans a package "delivered" but fails to actually deliver it to the buyer's address. This can prompt a variety of reactions from your buyer. Here is a suggested script for your response:

Dear [Customer],

I'm sorry you haven't yet received your item. The tracking result means that the Postal Service carrier who walks your route scanned the package and indicated he/she left it at your address. I can think of a few possible explanations why you haven't received it:

— The carrier left it at the wrong address and that person kept the package.

— The package was stolen after delivery.

— The carrier actually left the package on hold for you at the local post office but pressed the wrong button on his/her scanner and neglected to leave you a note indicating the package is at the post office.

Is it possible for you to ask the carrier about this? That is the quickest way to resolve this. If the package can't be found, please let me know and I'll assist you in obtaining a refund.

Best Regards,

Your Seller

- **Your return policy.** Decide on a return policy that you'll be able to explain consistently. You also need to comply with the federal mail order and telephone merchandise rule, also known as the "30-day rule" because it requires sellers to ship within the promised time frame or within a maximum of 30 days. In cases where the advertised product can't be delivered, the law requires sellers to notify the customer and offer the option of a full refund within seven days.

Many successful sellers have a more liberal return policy, and a good rule of thumb is to treat customers the way you expect to be treated. When a customer wants to return an item for a reason you don't consider 100 percent legitimate, give the customer the benefit of the doubt. Your time is much better spent finding and listing new items than in trying to learn if a problem buyer is unethical or just stupid.

Print online postage

For sellers shipping more than a few packages a week, an online postage service can save tremendous amounts of time. Instead of waiting in line at the Post Office, then waiting for the clerk to apply postage to all your packages, you print the postage yourself in a fraction of the time.

Using online postage enhances your record keeping by automatically building a file of all your mailings right on your computer. Records on each parcel shipped can be retrieved instantly—no rummaging through paper receipts. You also can purchase insurance online instead of waiting in line at the Post Office.

Some online postage plans allow you to print "stealth" postage, which hides the value of the postage. Instead, the label merely indicates the package weight and "U.S. Postage and Fees Paid." Since customers don't know the amount spent for postage, they are less likely to become irritated if the shipping and handling fee they paid is higher than the actual postage cost.

The online postage choices include:

- **eBay/PayPal.** PayPal and eBay users can print address labels that include postage for buyers using PayPal. No Postal Service account registration or software installation is needed. Stealth postage and insurance are available, as are pre-populated address fields.

  Fees. There is no monthly fee, but a processing fee of 20 cents is charged for each Media Mail, First Class, or Parcel Post label printed. There's no fee for Priority Mail or Express Mail labels.

- **Endicia.com.** Endicia enables users to print U.S. postage on an envelope, label, or piece of paper from your laser printer or a dedicated thermal label printer. Endicia is easy for beginners to use but also has advanced capabilities for high-speed batch printing when needed.

  Customer addresses can be imported from a database or copied from the clipboard. Users get free delivery confirmation on Priority Mail parcels. For Media Mail parcels, users get a discounted "electronic rate" for delivery confirmation compared with the "retail" fee when you pay at the Post Office.

  Endicia also enables users to purchase insurance from U-Pic Insurance Services, which offers more competitive rates than the Postal Service.

  Fees. Users pay $9.95 monthly or $99.95 annually for the basic plan, and $15.95 monthly or $174.95 annually for premium service. A 30-day free trial is available. The premium service includes more automation capabilities and the ability to print "stealth" postage.

- **Stamps.com.** Stamps.com's online postage service is similar to Endicia's but does not have the same range of features and support. Users can print stealth postage.

  Fees. Users pay $15.99 monthly.

- **Shipstream Manager,** www.pitneyworks.com/shipstream. Shipstream is offered by Pitney Bowes, which used to be a popular source from which to rent postage meters. The recently introduced Shipstream is its first Internet postage product that has the range of features required for businesses shipping parcels.

  Fees. Users pay $18.99 monthly.

- **Click-N-Ship,** www.usps.com/shipping/label.htm. The U.S. Postal Service enables online users to print shipping labels at this site. Registration is required for postage and batch label orders. At this time, postage may be printed only for Express Mail and Priority Mail labels.

- **USPS Shipping Assistant.** This free PC-based software distributed by the U.S. Postal Service creates shipping labels with delivery confirmation, signature confirmation, or Express Mail service. Users can receive discounted rates for Delivery Confirmation and Signature confirmation, and can calculate rates and send customers e-mail notification that the package is on the way, including the delivery confirmation number. Users must pay for postage separately. See www.usps.com/shippingassistant.

  Other resources. The Postal Service, UPS, and other carriers maintain several online resources that can help assess shipping options.

  Domestic Rate Calculators.

  USPS: http://www.usps.com/tools/calculatepostage

UPS: www.ups.com/using/services/rave/rate.html

International Rate Calculators.
International shippers may wish to consult these resources:
USPS: http://ircalc.usps.gov/
UPS: www.ups.com/using/services/rave/rate.html
DHL: www.dhl-usa.com/shipping/
FedEx: www.fedex.com/us/international

Organize your inventory

New sellers typically organize their merchandise by category or alphabetically. This works fine if your inventory consists of less than a few dozen items. But when your inventory becomes several hundred items or more, these offhand organizational techniques become impractical.

Let's see how a simple SKU (stock keeping unit) system can simplify your daily chores. With an SKU system, we'll identify each item with a unique number, which we'll affix to the item with a sticker.

Let's suppose your items are stored on two shelves. We'll call them Shelf A and Shelf B. The SKUs for items on Shelf A are A1, A2, A3, and so on. SKUs for items on the other shelf are B1, B2, B3, and so on.

Now, when you make a sale, instead of picking through the alphabet or rummaging through your shelves to find the right thing, you'll easily find the correct item by looking for its SKU sticker.

How much time can an SKU system save? A lot, depending on how large your inventory is. Let's assume that using SKUs saves you 45 seconds each time you pull an item off the shelf for an order. As your business grows, those 45 seconds add up. Suppose your business expands to the point where you're shipping 80 orders a day. Multiply the 45 seconds 80 times daily, and you're saving one hour per day. Multiply that hour five days per week, 52 weeks a year, and you've saved 32 eight-hour days, just by using a simple SKU system.

And the SKU system saves time not only when you pull items *off* the shelf but also when you put new inventory *on* the shelf. Instead of hunting down the right spot in the alphabet and reshuffling all your inventory, you'll put the new items in the first available spot, giving them the appropriate SKU for its position on the shelf.

In case you're not sold on SKUs yet, here's another benefit: After your inventory is more than a few hundred items, you're likely to accumulate multiple copies of some items. For example, let's say you have five Willie Mays baseball cards. Each card is unique by year of issue, photo, and condition. You don't want to accidentally send your run-of-the-mill card to the customer who ordered your top-notch card. If the cards have different SKUs, you won't make that mistake.

Design your SKU system. Now that we have a concept for an SKU system, how do we actually put it into practice? How does the SKU get into your listings and onto the label?

You can insert the SKU characters into your item's description. If you're using third-party software, this process can be automated.

A simple way to affix the SKU stickers to the items is to print the numbers on a sheet of removable Avery 5160 Labels. These small rectangular labels can be placed on the item so that the SKU is visible when you're facing the shelf. When you pick and pack the item for shipment, you can easily peel off the label, leaving no residue. (Be sure to use "removable" labels.)

You can write the SKUs on the labels by hand, or you can laser-print the whole sheet of 30 at once. If you know how to use Microsoft Word form letters, you can mail-merge your list of SKUs right onto the label sheet. You can download a free template to do this at www.avery.com.

Squeeze more profits

An eBay business can start out simply, but quickly become a technical challenge as your inventory and sales volume grow. Once you have a couple of dozen auctions running, you'll need a system for keeping track of the details. When Customer X sends a message asking when his item was shipped, you must be able to take care of the inquiry in just a moment. Otherwise, you'll quickly become bogged down with the minutia of day-to-day operations.

For many sellers, the answer is automation—software or an online service that helps manage the business. Fortunately, a number of innovative products and services have been introduced in the past few years that take the tedium out of eBay selling.

As we've seen, shaving a bit of time on repetitive tasks can have a big cumulative effect. Depending on your business, some of the products listed here could provide the same kind of benefits by automating the manual tasks you perform from your computer.

Some of these automation tools cost a lot of money, but can be worth it if they help make your eBay business more profitable. Consider whether these tools can help your bottom line in three important ways:

- Shaving the amount of time it takes for you to list an auction.

- Increasing the sales price of your average item.

- Boosting the number of your auctions.

Many of the tools made available for eBay sellers have been developed by computer programmers who happened to be sellers themselves. It makes sense that sellers invented these products, since they are most familiar with the specific challenges of running an eBay business.

Get efficient with fulfillment software

Try the evaluation versions of software when they are available, and test the responsiveness of the company's technical support. If the company isn't responsive when you make an inquiry before purchasing, you can assume they will not be of great help after they've collected your money.

You should also consider the risk of leaving the proper functioning of your business operations at the mercy of a small entrepreneurial company. Your business can be damaged severely if your vendor's system goes haywire and can't be fixed promptly. For example, what would happen to your business if eBay suddenly redesigned its system, and as a result, you could no longer use your vendor's software to manage your inventory or print packing slips? If history is any guide, you can count on this sort of thing happening periodically, so it's prudent to have a backup plan for how you'll operate when a vendor is down.

Some vendors faced with unexpected technical challenges have simply ceased operations, leaving their clients without service or refunds. In certain cases, payments may be recovered, but the larger issue is what happens to your business if it is held hostage to a service provider or piece of software that quits working.

If you're in the market for one of these services, check the vendor's Web site for testimonials from other reputable sellers. If you don't see any testimonials, ask the company for references. Any reputable company with a good product has no problem providing a list of happy clients.

Fees can add up quickly. Some vendors charge a modest one-time licensing fee for their software, but others want a cut of your monthly sales. Consider whether this fits with your business model. If your monthly gross on eBay is just a few hundred dollars now, a fee of 3 percent in exchange for the use of a nifty service might seem fair. But what if your business expands to the point that your monthly gross is $10,000? Will you think that $300 a month, $3,600 a year, is fair for using that software?

Before you commit to a fancy automation tool, you might consider what type of automation tools you can build yourself. If you're fairly computer-literate and can work with Microsoft Excel, you can devise your own method of automating order handling, for example. Therefore you might be able to get along just fine by using TurboLister, a free software listing tool provided by eBay.

For sellers who would rather use third-party software tools, below is a list of vendors that specialize in providing products for eBayers. In addition to the products and services listed here, you can consult the eBay Solutions Directory:

www.solutions.eBay.com

Also, you can consult the independent Web site Auction Software Review. Members can receive discounts on certain products and services and participate in forums:

www.auctionsoftwarereview.com

TurboLister. This free listing tool provided by eBay helps sellers create new listings and upload and edit them in bulk. You can search your listings in a variety of ways and the software provides toolbar and special views of your listings.

Cost: Free.

http://pages.ebay.com/turbo_lister/

File Exchange is an end-to-end bulk listing tool enabling high-volume sellers to list many items on eBay or Half.com by uploading a single file. Sellers can use flat files from Excel, Access, or other inventory software. Users can download active and sold listings.

Cost: Free.

http://pages.ebay.com/file_exchange/

Selling Manager is an online sales management tool provided by eBay for medium- and high-volume sellers. If you subscribe, the **All Selling** links in My eBay are replaced with **Selling Manager** links. Your eBay listings are split into "views," helping you manage your active and scheduled listings and post-sale tasks. Within views, you can search your listings for particular items and sort listings.

Cost: $4.99 per month for Basic Store subscribers.

http://pages.ebay.com/selling_manager/

Selling Manager Pro, also provided by eBay, adds additional features to Selling Manager. It supports higher volume sellers by providing more inventory and automation features. In addition to the Selling Manager features, the Pro version adds more views: Inventory, Reports and Selling Manager Pro Preferences.

Cost: $15.99 monthly for Featured and Anchored Store subscribers.

http://pages.ebay.com/selling_manager_pro/

ChannelAdvisor. ChannelAdvisor Pro is an eBay auction management service designed for individuals and small businesses. The service helps you organize and track your inventory, and create standardized auction listings. The service can also be used for eBay stores' fixed-priced listings.

Cost: ChannelAdvisor starts at $29.95 a month.

http://channeladvisor.com/

Blackthorne Pro is a desktop software product provided by eBay for larger-volume sellers. It supports businesses using multiple eBay seller IDs and uses a Microsoft Access database. Subscribers can create consignment plans and track suppliers. The Pro edition includes inventory management, reporting, and multiple user profiles.

Cost: $9.99 for Blackthorne, $24.99 for Blackthorne Pro.

Software for media sellers

These programs are designed for sellers of books, music and videos that have a numerical code assigned from the manufacturer such as an ISBN or UPC. These providers usually help automate selling at eBay, Half.com and other sites like Amazon.com.

Seller Engine. www.sellerengine.com

This PC software allows you to compare your prices with those of competing sellers without having to navigate to the Web page where your product is listed. The program can also be used to research prices of books and other media. By importing a list of ISBNs, the program can help you decide which books are worth the most money and worth your time to sell.

Fees. Users pay a monthly fee of $39.99. A free trial version of the software limits users to viewing 10 items at a time.

Bookrouter. www.bookrouter.com

Bookrouter enables booksellers to list their inventory on up to 19 online selling venues. Instead of having to upload inventory files to each site, Bookrouter automatically configures the data for each site. The service offers a way to adjust prices on different venues. You can raise or lower your prices by a percentage, a dollar amount, or a combination of those two factors on a site-by-site basis. Bookrouter also allows you to define a price range for books at various selling sites. It works with Amazon.com, ABAA/ILAB, Abebooks, Alibris, AntiQbook, Biblio.com, BiblioDirect, Bibliology, Biblion, Bibliophile, BookAvenue, Books&Collectibles, BookSellerSolutions, Choosebooks, Chrislands, Half.com, TomFolio, UsedBookCentral, and Wantedbooks.

Fees. Users pay $25 per month for up to five selling venues and $5 for each additional site. Bookrouter charges a one-time setup fee of

$50, which covers listing on up to five selling venues — additional sites cost $5 each. The setup fee covers testing a sample upload and trouble-shooting for each site.

Mail Extractor. www.mailextractor.com

Mail Extractor is an order fulfillment and inventory management program for booksellers using Half.com and Amazon. The software resides on your PC. The program parses the information contained in Amazon order fulfillment reports and in Half.com and PayPal/eBay e-mails to build packing slips and invoices. Users can send automated e-mail shipment notifications to buyers and manage inventory. Mail Extractor also automates the printing of postage for users of the Endicia online postage service.

Fees. Users pay a monthly fee that depends on how many items they have listed for sale — starting at $6.95 for up to 1,500 listings and climbing to $44.95 a month for sellers with more than 30,000 listings.

FillZ. www.fillz.com

FillZ is an online inventory and order management system for booksellers with a high volume of sales. Users can upload their inventory to many additional bookselling sites. Inventory levels are adjusted automatically at each selling site. FillZ supports Amazon, eBay Stores, Abebooks, Alibris, and others.

You can add inventory using a bar code scanner or your existing software. Fulfillment functions include generation of picklists and packing slips by location, SKU number, and order number. The software also generates shipment confirmation e-mails and works with different online postage services.

Fees. There is a minimum monthly fee of $50 for sellers with under $3,000 in monthly sales. Sellers with between $3,000 and $10,000 in monthly revenue are charged the $50 minimum plus 1 percent of their monthly sales revenue over $3,000. Sellers with more than $10,000 in monthly revenue are charged a $120 monthly fee plus 0.5 percent of monthly revenue over $10,000. Shipping fees aren't included in calculating a seller's monthly revenue.

FillZ charges eBay sellers a flat monthly fee of $5 plus $2 for each 1,000 uploaded records, which includes new listings, updates, and deletions.

The Art of Books. www.theartofbooks.com

The Art of Books is an online service that enables booksellers to manage their inventory across several selling venues from a single interface. It includes tools to automate order fulfillment, postage printing, inventory repricing, and pricing information via cell phone. Supported venues include eBay Stores, Amazon's U.S., Canadian, German, and U.K. sites; Alibris; Abebooks; and Half.com sellers with FTP accounts.

Fees. No fee is charged on the first $500 in monthly revenue, but users pay 1 percent of their monthly revenue between $500 and $10,000. A fee of 0.5 percent is paid on revenue over $10,000.

Monsoon. www.monsoonworks.com

Monsoon began offering three levels of online service for booksellers in 2005. The service automates several processes, such as listing inventory, adjusting prices, and managing customers. The service supports sellers using eBay Stores, Amazon Marketplace and six other bookselling venues. The company says its service can reprice up to 30,000 items per hour.

Fees. Monsoon asks that interested parties complete a signup form on their Web site because rates vary by the level of service a seller requires. Company representatives indicate that fees start at $199 for setup plus 3 percent of monthly sales.

BookWriter Web. www.bookwritersoftware.com

BookWriter Web is designed for booksellers who want to sell items on their own Web site. It automates the process of building Web pages to display your inventory. For booksellers who aren't interested in creating Web pages themselves, the company will customize a Web site for you for about $500.

Fees. Users pay a one-time licensing fee of $79 for BookWriter Web.

Research prices wirelessly

Many modern cell phones enable you to retrieve data over the Web. The services below enable you to check prices on marketplaces such as eBay, Half.com and Amazon by inputting ISBNs or UPCs. The services can help you decide which items are worth adding to your inventory. Depending on your wireless device, you may be able to connect a bar code scanner and avoid having to key in the ISBNs. The services access Amazon's Web Services platform, so the data is retrieved much faster and with less clutter than if you were browsing Amazon product pages.

ScoutPal. www.scoutpal.com

ScoutPal works with any Web-enabled cell phone or wireless PDA. You can also access prices from Amazon Marketplace, ABE, and PriceGrabber.com.

Fees. Users pay $9.95 monthly or $29.85 quarterly. A one-week free trial is available.

Bookhero. www.bookhero.com

Bookhero works with cell phones and wireless PDAs. It looks up pricing data on Amazon Marketplace. Up to 10 ISBNs can be retrieved in one request on a cell phone and up to 30 ISBNs on PDAs.

Fees. Users pay $8.95 monthly, $24.95 quarterly, or $89.95 annually.

AsellerTool. www.asellertool.com

AsellerTool looks up Amazon Marketplace prices for books, videos, and CDs using your cell phone, PDA, or PC. Users can retrieve data on up to nine items in one lookup operation. To keep waiting time to a minimum, the lookup result is limited to lowest used price, lowest new price, number of used listings, and the item's sales rank.

Fees. $4.99 a month. A seven-day free trial is available.

BookScout. www.theoldbookstore.com

This Web site operates a free cell phone lookup service. The company requires no fee but asks that you support it by purchasing items on Amazon.com through its referral link.

BookDabbler. www.bookdabbler.com

BookDabbler provides price and availability of new and used books at three levels of service, and offers a couple of options not available from other providers, including the ability to upload book wish lists.

Fees. Users pay a monthly fee of $5 to $9.95 depending on the service plan selected. A one-month free trial is available.

Market research tools

eBay offers a Marketplace Research product allowing you to view up to 90 days of eBay completed listings. The product allows you to:

- Analyze average selling prices and average start prices of items.
- Access charts that help you view trends in eBay buying and selling.
- Research top keyword searches on eBay by category and related keywords.

Three subscription levels are available, ranging from a two-day pass costing $2.99, a Basic subscription for $9.99 a month, and the Pro level costing $24.99 and providing access to the top searches on eBay. For more details, see:

http://pages.ebay.com/marketplace_research

eBay Sales Reports. eBay's Sales Reports is a free service enabling you to track your business's performance. You can measure your existing business against sales goals and discover areas of opportunity and possible improvement.

With Sales Reports, you can download data on your listed items, buyers, eBay fees, and metrics for each category. See:

http://pages.ebay.com/salesreports/welcome.html

Vendio provides several auction automation, store hosting, and market research tools. A few years ago, the company purchased **Andale**, a longtime provider of market research tools.

Vendio's research service enables you to determine the opening bid, reserve price, and listing format that yielded the best prices on eBay in the previous six months. It helps you discover the most successful products on eBay and the prices you can expect.

For more information, see:

http://www.vendio.com/services/research.html

Hammertap. This online service helps you determine how a product will sell and how much profit you can expect. You can research which days would be best for your auction, the best price to start your auction, and other ways to improve your business.

For more information, see:

http://www.hammertap.com/

Stay on eBay's good side

An efficient marketplace needs some regulation. eBay is a community governed by a variety of rules, and all sellers, large and small, must abide by those rules. The consequences for violations are the same for all types of sellers.

When sellers violate the eBay policies explained here, the consequences can include:

- Listing cancellation.

- Forfeit of eBay fees on canceled listings.

- Limits on account privileges.

- Loss of PowerSeller status.

- Account suspension.

Repeat offenders receive more severe sanctions. eBay's Trust & Safety team monitors the site for violations of community rules and accepts reports from eBay users through the Community Watch program.

- **Counterfeit items.** Counterfeit and knock-off items have proliferated onto many shopping venues, but these items are not only illegal, they're banned on eBay.

It may seem harmless enough to buy a fake Rolex watch or a pirated DVD from a downtown street vendor. But selling such items on eBay, even if you advertise the item as a "fake" or "replica," can get you booted from eBay and, potentially, in more hot water. The manufacturers of these products are understandably upset when sales of illegitimate knock-offs hurt their sales and profits, and the law is on their side.

If you're not certain that a "Gucci" bag you bought at a flea market is real, don't list it for sale on eBay. If you list a piece that you think looks like a Vuitton but is missing the label, don't describe it as a "Vuitton" in your listing. If you don't know what company made the item, don't compare it to a brand name. (Even if an item isn't a "fake," it's never kosher to compare it to another brand name in the title of your eBay listing. It is OK to compare its performance, but not appearance, to a brand name.)

Needless to say, sellers aren't allowed to sell unauthorized or "bootleg" copies of music, video or any other copyrighted work.

Sellers can't disclaim knowledge of whether an item is authentic. For example, if you're selling a painting and you don't know who the artist was, you can't state in your description, "Looks like it could be a Picasso, but I'm not sure. Bid accordingly."

For more information on copyright, trademark, and other intellectual property issues, consult eBay's Verified Rights Owner Program, or VERO:

http://pages.ebay.com/help/tp/programs-vero-ov.html

More eBay rules

Here are some more obscure eBay rules, but ignorance of them is no defense:

- **Unauthorized Faces, Names or Signatures.** Sellers aren't allowed to list an item with a photo or likeness, name, or signature of another person unless the product was made or authorized by that person.

- **False or Missing Contact Information.** Sellers and buyers are required to list accurate contact information such as name, address and/or telephone number when registering. Telephone numbers must not be a fax number or a disconnected number.

- **Writing original descriptions.** When listing an item for sale on eBay, you must describe it in your own words and use only those photos you've taken yourself. You can't copy the manufacturer's product description or logo from its Web site—doing so would violate copyright and trademark laws.

You can't copy another seller's listing description, but it's OK to state facts about your item that are similar to the way others have stated them. For example, if you're selling a radio, it's OK to copy the technical specifications from the manufacturer's Web site.

Prohibited and restricted items

eBay bans many items based on national and local laws, and also prohibits certain items that are legal but considered dangerous or in extremely poor taste. A good rule of thumb: If it's illegal to sell an item in your neighborhood—or you need a license to do so—the item is probably banned or restricted on eBay too.

If you sell internationally, remember that some items may be legal in your country but prohibited elsewhere.

Below is a list of many of the items prohibited by eBay. Some are flatly prohibited, while exceptions are made for some items. If you have any doubt about the suitability of an item, consult eBay's Web site to see exactly what is prohibited and what is allowed:

http://pages.ebay.com/help/policies/items-ov.html

- **Adult material.** Generally, materials unsuitable for persons under 18 are prohibited on eBay's main site. However, sales of certain items are permitted in eBay's **Everything Else: Mature Audiences** category. (See the below entry for Mature Audiences.)

- **Alcohol.** Exceptions are made for beverages in collectible containers when the value of the item is the container, not the beverage.

- **Animals and wildlife products.** No live animals, while some stuffed birds and the pelts and skins of some animals are permitted.

- eBay has a special code of conduct for the sale of **artwork**. Sellers must not knowingly sell unauthorized reproductions. When listing an exact replica painting, "reproduction" or "repro" must appear in the listing title, and the description must clearly state it's a reproduction.

- **Artifacts.** Do not sell original Native American crafts or items from caves or graves.

- **Catalytic converters and test pipes.** Certain catalytic converters are prohibited by the U.S. government.

- **Cell phone (wireless) service contracts.** Sellers must be an authorized reseller of cell phone services.

- **Charity or fund raising.** Listings must donate 10 percent of the sale to a recognized tax-deductible charity and have advance written permission from the nonprofit. A scanned copy of the consent letter must be included in your listing.

- **Used clothing.** Generally, clean used clothing is allowed. But eBay prohibits the sale of used underwear, including boxer shorts, panties, briefs, athletic supporters and diapers.

- **Coins.** Coins and paper money must be authentic and accurately described. See eBay's Web site for several restrictions on listing collectible coins.

- **Contracts.** For example, airline tickets are sold with terms that limit their transferability to second buyers. Be sure you have the right to resell an item.

- **Used cosmetics.** No used items whatsoever.

- **Counterfeit currency and stamps.**

- **Credit cards.** Must be expired 10 years previously.

- **Drugs and drug paraphernalia.**

- **Electronics equipment.** No radar detectors or devices enabling theft of paid TV signals.

- **Electronic surveillance equipment.** No products designed to secretly record private conversations.

- **Embargoed goods.**

- **Event tickets.** Some states prohibit the sale of tickets for more than their face value.

- **Firearms, weapons and knives.** Firearms and hand weapons are prohibited.

- **Food.**

- **Gift cards.** Can't exceed $500.

- **Government documents, IDs and licenses**

- **Hazardous, restricted, and perishable items.**

- **Human parts and remains.** No, you can't sell your liver—even if it's in good working order.

- **Items encouraging illegal activity.**

- **Lock-picking devices.**

- **Lottery tickets.**

- **Mailing lists and personal information.**

- **Manufacturers' coupons**

- **Mature content.** Adult materials are generally prohibited on eBay, but the sale of these items is allowed on eBay's main site: Pre-1980 Playboy, Playgirl and Penthouse magazines; video games rated

Mature; unrated DVDs that were issued with an MPAA rating; profanity if it's included in the original title or description of a DVD or CD; any media item included in eBay's pre-fill catalog.

The sale of the following types of items are restricted to eBay's **Everything Else: Mature Audiences** category: items requiring purchase by those 18 or older; items intended for sexual activity such as bondage, sadomasochism or similar acts; post-1980 Playboy, Playgirl, Penthouse and other adult magazines; movies rated X or intended for "Adult" viewers; AO-rated video games; and listings with images of frontal nudity or depicting any sexual activity, with limited exceptions.

Note that PayPal cannot be used to pay for items in eBay's Mature Audiences category.

- **Medical devices.**

- **Multilevel marketing, pyramid, matrix programs.** No programs where sellers receive proceeds from their own sales, as well as from sellers they recruit into the program.

- **Offensive material.** No items offensive to ethnic groups. No items that promote hatred, violence or intolerance toward racial or religious groups. For example, Nazi memorabilia is not allowed.

- **Pesticides.**

- **Plants (see Weeds and Seeds.)**

- **Police-related items.** No police identification or credentials. Unofficial, historical, and souvenir items are allowed.

- **Political memorabilia.** Sellers must follow terms of the "Hobby Protection Act," which regulates the sale of collectible items. See: **http://collectors.org/Library/Hobby_Protection_Act.asp**

- **Postage meters.**

- **Prescription drugs.**

- **Prohibited services.** No listings offering "virtual" relationships, no offers of a massage, sexual contact, date or escort.

- **Real estate.**

- **Recalled items.** No items identified by the U.S. Consumer Products Safety Commission as being hazardous.

- **Software.** Reselling software is allowed on eBay only in limited circumstances. Most software licenses restrict reselling after you've installed it on your computer. "Bundled" or OEM software can be sold with the original computer only. Also, eBay prohibits the sale of evaluation, test or beta software.

- **Slot machines.**

- **Stamps.**

- **Stocks and other securities.**

- **Stolen property, removed serial numbers.**

- **Surveillance equipment.**

- **Teacher's edition textbooks.** Solutions manuals for teachers and instructor manuals are prohibited. Student solutions manuals are permitted.

- **Tobacco.**

- **Transit- and shipping-related items.** For example, no aircraft operating manuals, no pilot or flight attendant uniforms.

- **Travel.** Sellers must be licensed travel agents authorized to conduct business nationwide who will personally book travel for winning bidders.

- **Weeds and seeds.**

- **Wine.**

More eBay no-nos

- **Shill bidding.** A seller's family, friends, roommates or employees are prohibited from bidding on that seller's auctions. This practice, called "shill bidding," distorts the bidding process by making demand appear greater than it really is, artificially increasing the final price.

To ensure your item doesn't sell at too low a price, use a reserve price or a higher starting price. Alternatively, you can use eBay's fixed-price format, which permits you to set a Buy It Now price.

If a seller is suspended for shill bidding, the suspension applies to all his eBay accounts. Suspended sellers aren't allowed to open new eBay accounts during the suspension or participate in bidding, buying or selling through any other means.

- **Keyword spamming.** When sellers use brand names or other keywords deemed inappropriate as a way of drawing attention to their item, they've violated eBay's keyword spamming policy. Any text you use in your listing's title or description must directly relate to the item you're selling.

For example, let's imagine you have a homemade leather case you use for carrying your Apple iPhone. If you list the item for sale and use either of those trademarked names, Apple or iPhone, that's considered keyword spamming. You can't use brand names in listings beyond the names used by the product's maker.

eBay's keyword spamming policy does not prohibit deliberate misspellings in listings. In fact, some sellers believe that shoppers are more likely to find items if the listing contains commonly misspelled words or synonyms that people might use in searching for such an item.

For example, let's imagine you're selling a ceramic beverage stein. You would not violate eBay rules by using the word "stine" in your title or description.

- **Diverting transactions.** Sellers are prohibited from asking customers to buy listed items outside eBay. The company frowns on this because it's a tactic for avoiding eBay selling fees, and it's a popular method for scammers too. Once your item is listed on eBay, you're obligated to sell it there. Your listing can't refer to your private Web site, off-eBay sales, or other buying venues. Sellers can, however, include links to their eBay Store, Store items, and their About Me page.

- **Spam** is prohibited on eBay, whether it is sent via e-mail, eBay's messaging system, or by Skype messaging. Spam is a message that is unsolicited and commercial in nature, mentioning the buying or selling of goods or services.

Sellers are, however, allowed to invite customers onto a mailing list, so long as the list is related to the transaction and the invitation to the mailing list isn't the primary purpose of the message.

- **Unreasonable shipping & handling fees.** This is a sensitive area for buyers, and it's a leading cause for negative feedback. Fees for shipping and handling should cover "reasonable" costs for postage and packaging materials. Shipping & handling can't be listed using a percentage of the selling price.

Don't play games with your buyers. Don't sell a lightweight item for $1 then charge $8 for shipping. If it comes to the attention of eBay, they'll close your auction on the grounds of "fee circumvention" since you've avoided paying a final value fee on most of your proceeds.

If postage or shipping fees cost $4, a shipping and handling fee of $5 or $6 is considered reasonable. Sellers aren't allowed to add surcharges for accepting certain forms of payment such as checks, money orders, credit cards or electronic funds transfers. These costs are expected to be included in your item's price.

- **Fee Circumvention.** eBay prohibits sellers from using any techniques to avoid paying eBay's regular seller fees. This includes:

  - **Off eBay Offer.** Sellers can't use eBay listings to advertise how to buy the item outside eBay. Likewise, e-mail addresses, phone numbers and domain names cannot be used in eBay listing titles, subtitles or images.

●**Catalog Sales.** Sellers aren't allowed to list catalogs enabling buyers to order items directly. In other words, sellers can't offer a catalog for a low bid price, then encourage sales from the catalog outside eBay. (This policy does not prevent the sale of old, collectible catalogs from which items can no longer be ordered.)

●**Want ads, trades.** eBay prohibits listings that express the desire to buy or trade items. Listings must describe an item for sale. Such advertisements are permitted only within eBay's **Want it Now** area.

● **Payment Surcharges.** Sellers can offer a discount to buyers who use a preferred payment method, but are not allowed to charge buyers additional fees for using any ordinary payment form—PayPal, checks, money orders, credit cards or bank transfers.

● **Miscategorization.** Listing items outside their appropriate category when they should appear in a flat fee category (such as vehicles and homes) constitutes Fee Circumvention.

● **Requiring additional purchases.** Items that require the purchase of an additional item aren't allowed. Additional warranties and services (such as local installation of a ceiling fan) are permitted. But the optional warranty or service must be directly related to the item and can't do any of the following:

●Alter the value of the item "substantially."

●Be an "additional" item.

●Be priced "excessively."

●Cause the listed item to have an artificially low price. For example, listing a camcorder for sale at a Buy It Now price of $1 but selling its battery separately at $100 would violate eBay's rule.

● **Choice listings.** eBay doesn't allow sellers to create listings where buyers select from a list of items. For example, if you were individually selling quilts, you'd need to create a separate listing for each one; a listing that pictured all the quilts and asked customers to choose one would violate the rules.

Likewise, listings stating "highest bidder gets first choice" aren't allowed, and listings can't be "subject to availability." You can't ask buyers to contact you to check which colors, styles or quantities are available.

Two exceptions to this rule: listings that offer custom-made items or services or multiple quantity fixed-price listings, where a choice of color is allowed when the items are otherwise the same.

eBay enforces this rule to ensure that buyers receive exactly what they expected, and to prevent sellers from circumventing eBay fees and offering transactions outside eBay.

- **Reserve price misuse.** Sellers aren't allowed to misuse eBay's Reserve price feature, defined as:

  - Asserting that a bidder is required to purchase your item even if the reserve price wasn't met.

  - Avoiding reserve fees by canceling bids and ending your listing early because your desired price hasn't been met.

- **Restrictions on bonuses, prizes, giveaways, raffles.** eBay doesn't permit listings that promote giveaways, sweepstakes, raffles or prizes because such promotions are closely regulated by local governments and are illegal in some areas. Also prohibited are bonus listings where a seller doesn't state the exact amount that triggers the bonus, or Multiple Item listings that don't offer precisely the same bonus to all buyers.

- **Seller Non-Performance.** If more than 5 percent of a seller's customers are dissatisfied (according to feedback and Item Not Received complaints over the previous 90 days), it's a violation of eBay's Seller Non-Performance policy.

Stay on Uncle Sam's good side

If you're running a business, you need good records to prepare your tax returns competently. You must support the income, expenses, and credits you report on your return. Generally, these are the same records you use to monitor your business and prepare your financial statements.

Business records must be available in case the Internal Revenue Service demands an inspection at any time. If the IRS asks for an explanation of your tax returns, complete records will help conclude the examination quickly.

In addition to staying on the right side of the law, keeping good business records will help you manage your business more effectively through these critical tasks:

- **Monitoring your business's progress.** Records will show whether your business is improving or faltering, where sales are coming from, and what changes in your practices might be appropriate. Good records give you a better chance of making your business succeed.

- **Preparing financial statements.** Good records are essential for preparing accurate financial statements. These statements can aid in any necessary dealings with your bank and creditors, as well as help you make business decisions.

- **Identifying receipt sources.** Your business will have money and goods coming in from various sources, and you'll need to keep this information separate from personal receipts and other income.

Your business's legal structure

If you decide to pursue eBay selling as a regular endeavor, you'll need to decide how your business will be formally organized and how you'll meet your tax obligations. As your business grows, you should periodically revisit the question of the best form of organization for your business.

- **Sole proprietorship.** Establishing a sole proprietorship is cheap and relatively simple. This term designates an unincorporated business that is owned by one individual, the simplest form of business organization to start and maintain. You are the sole owner and you take on all the business's liabilities and risks. You state the income and expenses of the business on your own tax return.

Any business that hasn't incorporated is automatically a sole proprietorship. So if you haven't incorporated, formed a partnership, or established a limited liability company, your business is a sole proprietorship by default.

The good news about a sole proprietorship is that you're entitled to all the profits from the business. On the other hand, you are 100 percent responsible for all debts and liabilities. So if your business is sued, your personal assets could be seized.

As a sole proprietorship, you're liable for paying income tax and self-employment tax (Social Security and Medicare taxes), and for filing quarterly estimated taxes based on your net income. Since you don't have an employer reporting your income and withholding a portion of your paycheck for taxes, you must inform the IRS about the income from your eBay selling and make quarterly tax payments on the profits. Quarterly installments of the estimated tax, submitted with Form 1040-ES, are due April 15, June 15, September 15, and January 15 of the following calendar year. If you don't yet sell full-time and you also work at a job where your employer withholds income for taxes, you can ask your employer to increase your withholding. That way you might avoid having to mail in quarterly estimated payments on your profits.

As far as the IRS is concerned, a sole proprietorship and its owner are treated as a single entity. Business income and losses are reported with your personal tax return on Form 1040, Schedule C, "Profit or Loss From Business."

If you've never filed a Schedule C with the IRS before, you might wish to hire an accountant to assist you with the first year's return. The following year you might complete the return yourself. One helpful tool in this regard is tax-preparation software such as TurboTax or TaxCut. Unlike the IRS instruction pamphlets, these products guide you through the tax-filing process in plain English. The program can save you several hours at tax time because you don't have to decipher the arcane language of the IRS.

- **Partnership.** A partnership is the relationship between two or more persons who agree to operate a business. Each person contributes something toward the business and has a stake in its profits and losses. Partnerships must file an annual information return to report the income and deductions from operations. Instead of paying income tax, the partnership "passes through" profits or losses to the partners, and each partner includes their share of the income or loss on their tax return.

- **Corporation.** In a corporation, prospective shareholders exchange money or property for the corporation's stock. The corporation generally takes deductions similar to those of a sole proprietorship to calculate income and taxes. Corporations may also take special deductions.

- **Limited liability company.** A limited liability company (LLC) is a relatively new business structure allowed by state statute. LLCs are popular because owners have limited personal liability for the company's debts and actions, as is also the case for a corporation.

Local ordinances

Call your county government's headquarters to ask what types of permits and licenses are required for your business. Some cities, counties, and states require any business to get a business license. If you're working at home, your city or county may require a "home occupation permit" or a zoning variance, and you might have to certify that you won't have walk-in retail customers. Since your business is an online and mail-order business, this shouldn't be a problem.

If you are conducting your business under a trade name or your eBay ID, you should file a "fictitious name" certificate with your county or state government office so people who deal with your business can find out who the legal owner is. This is also known as a DBA name (Doing Business As) or an "assumed name."

• **Sales taxes.** Although the Internet is a "tax-free zone" in many respects, this does not apply to state sales taxes for goods sold to customers in your state. To pay the tax, you'll need to open an account and obtain a "resale license," known as a resale number or sales tax certificate in some instances.

You don't collect state sales tax on orders shipped outside your state, however. This is because Internet sales, as well as fax, telephone, and mail-order sales, shipped to another state aren't subject to sales tax unless you have an office or warehouse located there. In some states, shipping and handling fees are not subject to sales tax, but in some they are—you will need to investigate the issue for your home state. This is the way things operate today, but there's no guarantee it will stay this way.

Once you've made the decision that your eBay business is no longer a hobby, obtain a resale certificate from your state tax office. This will relieve you of paying state sales tax on the items you buy for resale, but it will also obligate you to report and pay taxes on the sales you make to customers within your state.

A caveat: State sales taxes are an evolving area you'll need to monitor. Because online sales are growing so rapidly, local governments are salivating at the prospect of collecting local sales taxes from eBay sellers, no matter where the item is shipped. Sooner or later, it's inevitable that eBay sellers will be regulated and taxed more than they are today.

- **eBay Checkout's tax table.** An easy way to collect your required sales taxes is to use eBay Checkout's tax table, where you can specify the rate and state where you charge tax. Buyers who visit your listing will see the appropriate tax rate. When the buyer pays using eBay Checkout, the correct tax is calculated and displayed based on the shipping address, and is included in the total.

If your state requires you to charge sales tax on your shipping and handling charges, you can select the check box labeled **Also charge sales tax on S&H.**

- **Income taxes.** Your form of business determines which income tax return form you have to file. For the vast majority of sellers without employees or a walk-in store, a sole proprietorship makes the most sense. As noted previously, the other most common forms of business are partnerships, corporations, and limited liability companies.

Many beginning sellers spend lots of time dreaming about what they'll be able to "write off" on their tax return, now that they have a business. Actually, what you're doing is paying taxes on your net profits. Your write-offs are the costs of doing business, such as buying inventory and paying for postage. What's left over is the profit, and you pay income tax on that.

As far as the IRS is concerned, your business must become profitable within three years or it will be considered a hobby, and none of the expenses will be deductible. For example, your mileage traveling to estate sales is deductible for tax purposes. But don't rely on your memory to keep track of such expenses. Keep a notebook in your car to document the mileage and expenses for your buying trips. If you're ever audited, the IRS will want to see documentation for your travel and other deducted expenses.

To figure your taxes, you'll need to keep track of every penny involving your business. Keep receipts and records, and put your expenses into categories such as "postage," "shipping supplies," "inventory," and so on.

Your bookkeeping chores can be greatly simplified with financial software such as Quicken. Most banks offer free downloads of your transactions, and once you set it up, Quicken can automatically categorize all your business expenses and eliminate most of the headaches at tax time. If you have a debit or check card linked to your account, you can use the card for nearly all your business transactions. Those records can be downloaded into Quicken right along with your banking records, making your bookkeeping that much simpler.

If you're familiar with bookkeeping and accounting principles, you might be able to do a better job with QuickBooks software, which is designed especially for small-business accounting.

- **Supporting documents.** The law doesn't require any particular record-keeping technique, as long as you can plainly show your income and expenses. Your records must summarize your business transactions, showing your gross income, deductions, and credits. It's a good idea to have a separate checking account for your business so that your personal funds are not included.

You should preserve the paper trail of any purchases, sales, and other transactions, including any invoices or receipts, sales slips, bills, deposit slips, and records of canceled checks. Keep documents that support your tax return organized and in a secure place. More detailed information is available in IRS Publication 583, "Starting a Business and Keeping Records."

- **Business use of your home.** You may be able to deduct expenses related to the business use of parts of your home. This deduction is subject to certain requirements and doesn't include expenses such as mortgage interest and real estate taxes.

To qualify to claim expenses for business use of your home, you must use part of your home exclusively and regularly as your principal place of business or for storage. This means the area used for your business must be a room or other separate identifiable space, but you are not required to designate the space by a permanent wall or partition.

There are some exceptions to the "exclusive use" test. If you use part of your home for storage of inventory, you can claim expenses for the business use of your home without meeting the exclusive use test — but you must meet these criteria:

- Your business is selling wholesale or retail products.

- You keep the inventory in your home for use in your business.

- Your home is your business's only fixed location.

- You use the storage space on a regular basis.

- The space used for storage is a separately identifiable space suitable for storage.

To qualify under the regular use test, you must use a specific area of your home for business on a regular basis. "Incidental" or "occasional" business use is not regular use as far as the IRS is concerned.

- **Insurance.** Home-based businesses aren't usually covered under a regular homeowners or renter's insurance policy. If inventory items are stolen or damaged, it's probably not covered. If a delivery person or customer is injured at your home, you may be liable unless an "endorsement" or "rider" is added to your homeowner's or renter's policy. The cost of the additional premium is usually quite low for a business without employees or a huge inventory, so it's well worth considering.

- **Bookkeeping.** For a small eBay business, simple "cash basis" bookkeeping should suffice. The cash method entails recording income when money is received and expenses as they are paid. "Cash basis" does not necessarily mean your transactions are in cash, but refers to checks, money orders, and electronic payments as well as currency. If you're not familiar with the basics of bookkeeping, read *Small Time Operator: How to Start Your Own Business, Keep Your Books, Pay Your Taxes and Stay Out of Trouble* by Bernard Kamoroff.

Cash accounting is simpler to understand and use than the other type of bookkeeping, accrual accounting. Businesses are allowed to use cash accounting if annual sales are below $1 million.

- **Hiring employees.** The decision to begin hiring employees is a big step for any business. Although employees can enable you to expand your selling and profits, hiring will add tremendously to your paperwork and the extent to which your business is regulated by the government. Having employees means that you need to keep payroll records and withhold income, Social Security, and state taxes, as well as Medicare and worker's compensation insurance. The states and the IRS require timely payroll tax returns and strict observance of employment laws. Penalties are usually swift and severe for failure to pay payroll taxes.

An eBay seller struggling with a busy workload might be tempted to pay cash "under the table" for help instead of actually hiring employees during their transition from a one-person shop to employer status. Don't do it. There is no gray area here—such practices are illegal because payroll taxes and worker's compensation insurance aren't being paid.

An alternative to taking on employees is to hire independent outside contractors. You can hire contractors as needed, and the practice entails less paperwork and none of the headaches of paying employment taxes or producing payroll tax returns.

If you hire an independent contractor, make certain the person doing the work understands completely that they are not an employee. Numerous small-business owners have gotten into scrapes with state and federal regulators when their independent contractors were later denied unemployment compensation or were found not to have paid their own Social Security taxes.

Make friends, sell more

No matter what kind of business you have, its success depends on two things: It must serve a need, and you must find customers.

Most new businesses fail simply because too few customers found them. On eBay, that problem is pretty much solved for you; there's a critical mass of buyers already shopping there. But you can improve your results on eBay—and on your own Web site—by taking advantage of some recent innovations. These community-building tools are sometimes called Web 2.0, and include things like blogs and product reviews. But whatever you want to call this marketing tactic—buzz, word of mouth, social media, peer-to-peer or viral marketing—it works well for eBay sellers because it's free advertising. In fact, it's better than advertising.

And fortunately, there is a very straightforward, ethical way of gaining this free exposure: by using these social networking tools, both on eBay and outside eBay on networks such as MySpace. And unlike most traditional advertising, social networking can pay dividends for years to come because it forges a strong link between you and consumers, enabling your biggest fans to become evangelists for your business. It's the same as having a "street team" pounding the pavement for you. Just as your street team might pass out fliers about a show or new product, your MySpace friends can forward the same type of information using electronic messages to a much larger audience.

Entrepreneurs can no longer depend on interruption-based ads, such as commercials and junk mail, which force consumers to stop what they're doing and pay attention. But with social networking, you can influence these consumers precisely at the point where they're engaged.

With these powerful new tools, it's important to learn the ropes because marketing with social media is a double-edged sword. A single member of the community you're targeting has a voice just as loud as yours. Yes, if the community likes you, they'll help spread the word about you better than a million-dollar ad campaign. On the other hand, one disgruntled customer might be even more motivated—and effective—in badmouthing you.

- **Write an eBay Guide.** If you have a niche on eBay—any type of product you sell regularly and are knowledgeable of, like antique clocks, '60s memorabilia, or the latest electronic gadgets—you can spread your reputation as an expert in that field by writing an eBay Guide.

This is a relatively new feature at eBay, but increasingly popular. In the text of your guide, you can include photos and links to eBay pages and eBay searches. You can also add keywords, known as **tags**, which will help buyers find your guide. For example, a guide about collector's glassware might include the tags "glass," "stemware," "crystal," and "vintage tableware."

Lisa Cataudella, an attorney who sells used fashion items on eBay part-time, wrote one of the site's most frequently viewed guides. She spent about 20 minutes writing the guide, "How to spot a fake Coach bag," based on her years of experience in buying and selling those items. Her guide lists 16 tips on how to recognize a knock-off by looking at the fabric, zipper, stitching and other clues. The URL for the guide is below, but you can probably find it faster by Googling this: "ebay guides how to find a fake coach bag."

http://reviews.ebay.com/How-to-spot-a-fake-COACH-bag_W0QQugidZ10000000000839005

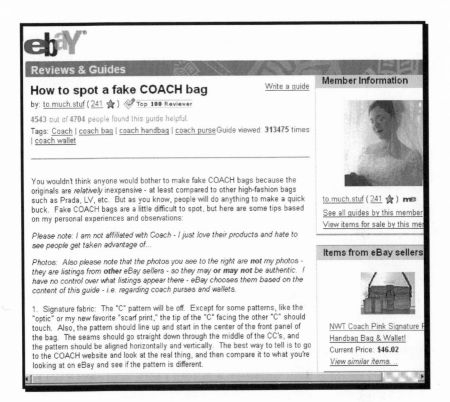

The 20 minutes Cataudella spent writing her guide has paid off—big time. It's been viewed 260,000 times, funneling thousands of shoppers to her eBay listings. And she's gotten lots of satisfaction from being able to help other eBayers be smart shoppers.

"I receive at least five e-mails per day asking for my advice, both from buyers and sellers," Cataudella said. "Most everyone is very grateful, and so they consider me a trusted seller."

eBay guides can bring you new customers in a couple of ways. Readers can click on your User ID and immediately begin browsing your inventory. Also, a link to your listings of related merchandise can show up right there on your guide's Web page.

Your guide can garner valuable exposure to new customers too, not just regular eBayers. Because the guides are indexed by Google and other search engines, when people search the Web for information like that in your guide, there's a good chance these searchers will discover you and your merchandise, regardless of whether they're current eBay members.

You can read more guides or begin writing one yourself here:

http://reviews.ebay.com/

Another way to get started is to search for a product you want to review. On the item page, scroll down to the section called "Item Specifics." Click on **See Reviews**, then **Write a review.**

• **Get Wiki.** You may have heard about the wildly popular online encyclopedia called Wikipedia, where anyone can write or edit the articles. eBay has something similar, called the eBay Wiki. It's a dynamic set of articles written and maintained by eBay buyers and sellers. You can add an article on any topic or about any product. Any eBay member is allowed to edit the information in any article. For more information, see:

http://www.ebaywiki.com/

• **eBay Groups.** Groups are sets of eBay buyers and sellers with a common interest. By joining or forming a group, you can participate in discussions, polls, newsletters and calendars pertaining to the group. See:

http://groups.ebay.com

Profit with stunts and gimmicks

Through the years, all sorts of zany eBay auctions have caught the public's imagination and become fodder for water-cooler chatter. The resulting notoriety can send millions of viewers to an auction, boost bidding through the roof, and earn the seller publicity that can't be bought with any amount of money.

Ad space on swimsuit model Shaune Bagwell's cleavage was auctioned on eBay. The winning bid was $15,099 from GoldenPalace.com, an online casino.

One particularly memorable action was for a toasted cheese sandwich that supposedly looked like an image of the Virgin Mary. Another auction offered seats on a mission to find Amelia Earhart's lost plane. One guy even offered to auction his liver (until eBay shut down the listing.) A shapely female model sold advertising space on her chest. The buzz about imaginative listings like these can spread like wildfire, and the hottest ones can be written up in newspapers around the globe. Talk about free advertising!

Now there's a community-driven mechanism to get the word out about the best notable auctions, called **Best of eBay**. The purpose is to showcase the most popular and eccentric listings, drawing more attention to the listings and eBay itself. Buyers and sellers nominate the listings, vote on them, and discuss them. Here's how it works:

- **Nominate Listings.** Any eBay member can nominate listings they think are fun or unusual. Click the **Nominate to Best of eBay** button to begin.

- **Place Votes.** Vote for your favorite listings and watch them rise to the top. Click on **Vote for this Item** on the right of each item.

- **Chime in.** Add comments to your Best of eBay nominations and share your favorites by using the **Email to a Friend** link near the bottom of the listings.

For more information, see:

http://bestof.ebay.com/

- **eBay neighborhoods.** eBay is allowing members to create "neighborhoods" organized around certain types of merchandise.

You can create a neighborhood yourself to pull together listings, reviews, guides, blogs, and discussion posts related to whatever you want. It's a pretty neat "social shopping" idea, and you can probably see how a seller could tap this feature for free advertising. For example, if you were selling a first edition of a book signed by J.K. Rowling, you could come right to a Harry Potter neighborhood and post your details to the discussion board. And since the eBay members congregating here are Potter fans, your free exposure here would probably be more valuable than a listing on eBay's home page—and without the listing upgrade fee!

Erik and Carla Schneider auctioned their wedding ring to raise money for the anti-hunger charity Hope Equity. The winning bid was $5,125.

The possibilities for using this Neighborhoods feature are endless. Whatever you're an expert on, start a neighborhood about it.

To get your reviews, guides, and blog posts to appear in certain neighborhoods, you'll need to have content related to that neighborhood. If your content doesn't appear where you think it should, try adding more related keywords within your guides, reviews or blog. For example, if your neighborhood is the New York Jets, then add more football, NY Jets, or Jets-related terms.

To suggest a new neighborhood:

- Click the **Suggest** link.

- Enter a name for the neighborhood.

- Type a short description of the neighborhood.

- Enter keywords related to your neighborhood.

- Write about why you think the neighborhood is important.

- Click **Submit.**

Tag, you're it!

Tagging is a relatively new but increasingly popular way for Internet users to organize things by using personal keywords. Tags can be used to label all kinds of items found on the Web, including Web pages, product reviews, pictures and videos. Already, some are calling tags the Internet's Dewey Decimal System.

Users create tags for their own purposes, but they can be used by anyone. With enough people participating, tags can become an effortless, super-accurate recommendations system among like-minded people. The site that popularized tagging was **www.Flickr.com**, a social site where users store, organize and share their digital photos. Instead of using a single category for organizing pictures—like a folder labeled "2005 Vacation"—members use one- or two-word tags like waterfall, solar eclipse, Houston, Joe or 2005. This way, photos can be grouped and discovered in multiple ways.

Tags are a form of *metadata*, which means, literally, "data about data." Tagging creates a *folksonomy*, a bottom-up method of categorization. *Taxonomies* are governed by experts like librarians and botanists who want to show hierarchical relationships. Folksonomies are built by amateurs but can be more helpful for users. Increasingly, people use tags to tap collective wisdom.

- **Tag-based marketing.** As a marketer, you should use tags to stay current on how people are finding and sharing information in your field. You can subscribe to RSS feeds to monitor how consumers tag information related to your area of business. For example, to keep tabs on antique watches, you could bookmark this page:

http://del.icio.us/tag/antique+watches

- **eBay tags.** For sellers, eBay tags might best be thought of as "search engine bait" you can embed in your blogs, reviews and guides. By using tags effectively, you can lure more buyers to your listings— and those buyers will be coming from everywhere, from eBay and outside eBay.

For example, if you're a seller who specializes in political memorabilia, you'll want to seed your eBay blogs, guides and reviews with tags like "campaign pins," "political posters," "presidential campaign," "Lincoln," and so on—whatever you're an expert on and whatever you're selling.

You've got to use tags with real content; otherwise your tags can be viewed as spam. It's against eBay's rules to use tags that aren't relevant to the content you post on eBay and the products you sell. If your tags are deemed inappropriate or considered "keyword spam," they're subject to removal.

For an example on how to do this right, take a look at this guide by eBay seller Adam Nash about selling presidential $1 coins:

http://reviews.ebay.com/Collecting-the-New-Presidential-1-Dollar-Program-Coins_W0QQugidZ10000000002485987

Near the bottom of the page is a list of "related tags" such as gold, First Spouse, US coins, Bullion and Dollar Coins. Clicking on these tags takes you to pages containing similar tags. Likewise, an eBay member might discover Nash's guide by searching for any of those tags.

You create your tags as you write your blogs, reviews and guides, and you can always edit, delete or add new ones later. Each piece of content you post on eBay can feature up to 10 tags, with each tag containing a maximum of four words.

- **My World.** Most of your eBay community features are gathered into a space called My World, and each member has a unique URL: http://myworld.ebay.com/your-user-id. Replace the characters "your-user-id" with your eBay ID.

My World gives you a customizable, personal area for content such as:

- Links to your items.
- Photos of you.
- Highlights from your eBay blog.
- A guest book where visitors can leave comments and notes.

You can customize your My World page by changing the settings and style this way:

- Go to your My World URL and sign in.
- Click **Add Content** to add or delete modules.
- Click **Change Layout** to remove modules.
- Click **Change Style** to change your page colors.

Get buzz

Undoubtedly you've heard of MySpace, which is most famous as an online hangout for teens. What you might not know is that MySpace is also populated by millions of eBay buyers and sellers who use it as a networking tool. Anyone who wants to promote themselves or their business can do so for free on MySpace.

New "profiles" are created daily for eBay sellers, artists, restaurants, movies, TV shows, bars, towns, your next-door neighbor, and nearly any other entity imaginable. Used wisely, MySpace can provide genuine word of mouth for your eBay business and find you some new friends to boot.

MySpace and other popular networks such as Facebook certainly aren't mandatory for eBay sellers. If you're already snowed under with selling tasks, don't feel guilty if you don't have time to throw yourself into social networking this year. But keep it in the back of your mind.

Marketing experts believe this is the future of online selling and communication. If you have some time to dabble with it, it sure won't hurt, and you just might have some fun, too.

In 2006, barely two years after its launch, MySpace became the most popular U.S. Web site based on number of visits. With nearly 100 million members, every target market is represented, already sliced and diced by interests and geography. Each MySpace member has his or her own circle of like-minded friends. After you become someone's MySpace "friend," you have access to his or her friends. And each of your new friends has more friends.

While there are hundreds of social-networking sites—Facebook, Friendster, Orkut and Tribe.net, to name just a few—MySpace has captured the lion's share of the traffic. To get started visit **www.MySpace.com** and click the "Sign Up" box on the right.

If you wish, you can make your MySpace account private until you're ready to use it. Go to **Account Settings** and then **Privacy Settings**.

MySpace? You might be thinking, "Isn't that for high-school kids?" Sure, that's the stereotype; MySpace is popular with kids. But with nearly 100 million members and the No. 1 traffic rank on the entire Internet, clearly there's more to it than loitering schoolkids.

In addition to its potential for promoting your business, MySpace is a wickedly good research tool. For example, in about 10 seconds you can find out how many members say Jimmy Buffet is their favorite singer, or something from the "Harry Potter" series is their favorite book. You can zap a message to any of these folks, or you can quickly locate members in your ZIP code who are science-fiction buffs. MySpace as a research tool can produce the same results as an expensive, traditional direct mail campaign—and it's free. How you use this tool to further your business is limited only by your imagination.

Making friends on MySpace

There are several ways to find people on MySpace who might be in your target market—by searching for *postcards, quilts, depression glass,* or whatever specialty you're in. Once you've found potential friends, you can send a request for them to "add" you as a friend. The invitee can accept, decline, or ignore your request, although most people accept.

Once you're friends with someone on MySpace, you can post comments on each other's profile pages and see each other's full circle of friends. Here's how to find friends and potential readership on MySpace:

- **Browse friends' lists of members interested in your field.** Find the MySpace profiles of members who share similar businesses goals and target markets. On the right side, scroll down a bit to the link **See All of [Name]'s Friends**. Start sending invitations—you'll get many potential customers this way. Here's another twist: Send an invitation to a famous business operator, and if they accept, post a comment, which appears on the bottom right of their MySpace page. More exposure for you.

- **Search.** Click **Search** on the top toolbar on the MySpace home page. You can limit your search to certain areas such as Blogs, Music Interest, Books Interest, or others. Let's imagine you're looking for MySpace members interested in autographed baseballs. Click on **Search** and enter "autographed baseballs." Presto, you've got a list of every MySpace member who's used the words "autographed baseballs" in that part of their profile. Also try the **Affiliations for Networking** search tool a bit farther down the page.

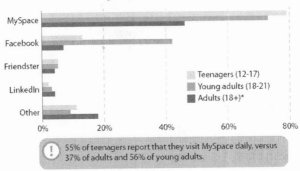

MySpace Dominates Social Networking Usage, With Facebook A Distant Second

Percentage who use site at least weekly:

Legend:
- Teenagers (12-17)
- Young adults (18-21)
- Adults (18+)*

> 55% of teenagers report that they visit MySpace daily, versus 37% of adults and 56% of young adults.

Base: US online social networking site users

Source: Forrester's NACTAS Q4 2006 Youth Media & Marketing And Finance Online Survey
*Source: Forrester's NACTAS Q3 2006 Media & Marketing Online Survey

---

Social Networking Site Users Represent An Attractive And Viral Audience

Adult social networking site user demographics and psychographics

	Adult social networking site users	Site usage daily or more	Interested in marketer profiles
Mean age	37	32	33
Male	52.9%	52.8%	53.3%
Average household income (US$)	$63,390	$61,688	$63,595
College degree or higher	33%	28%	27%
Gen X (27-40)	43%	45%	49%
Read blogs weekly or more	34%	50%	50%
Publish own blog weekly or more	21%	39%	35%
Average number of social network sites used weekly or more	0.79	1.38	1.26
"I am a natural leader — people always listen to my opinion"*	33%	32%	49%
"I often tell my friends about products that interest me"*	50%	47%	61%
"I like to show off my taste and style"*	14%	18%	27%

Base: US adult online social network users
*Percentage of respondents who agree with this statement
Source: Forrester's NACTAS Q3 2006 Media & Marketing Online Survey

Illustrations reprinted with permission from "Marketing on Social Network Sites" by Charlene Li, Forrester Research Inc., July 2007.

- **Browse for friends.** If you serve a local clientele through your eBay business, it's useful to browse for potential MySpace friends by geographic area. On the home page, click **Browse** and the **Advanced** tab. You'll be able to view member profiles within a specified distance of postal ZIP Codes, as well as other criteria such as age, gender, religion, and income. Many single MySpace members use this feature to look for potential dates, but it's also useful for eBayers who want to drum up local business.

- **Browse comments on other member profiles.** Comments from MySpace friends appear on the bottom right of profile pages. The most recent comments appear at the top, accompanied by the comment writer's photo or image. Members who leave these comments tend to be the most active and vocal MySpace users, and make good friends. In particular, seek out people who've posted thoughtful comments, like "Enjoyed seeing your profile and getting more information." Skip messages such as, "You ROCK, Man!!!"

- **Sending friends requests.** Once you find a potential friend, click **Add to Friends** under their profile's main photo on the left. And if you want to increase the odds of making a real connection, don't stop there—send a personalized message by clicking the **Send a Message** link. It requires some extra work, but you can't convert "friends" into customers simply by pecking on your mouse button.

- **Accepting friends.** Once you've done some networking on MySpace, people will start seeking you out. But don't feel obligated to accept anyone and everyone. Click to their profile page first, and make sure their interests are in line with yours.

There are two ways of approaching MySpace friendships: trying to acquire as big a list as possible, or having a smaller group you can make stronger connections with individually. In any case, the people who ultimately become customers will be those in your core groups, those who feel a connection.

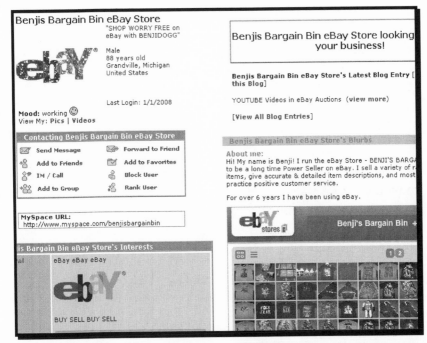

The MySpace profile for eBay seller Benjis Bargain Bin links directly to the seller's store. See http://www.myspace.com/benjisbargainbin

- **Create an "event."** Having a clearance sale? Announce it to your MySpace friends by creating a MySpace event and sending electronic invitations. To get started, simply click **Events** on the top navigation bar on any MySpace page, then **Create New Event**. Your "event" can be a yard sale at your house, or it can be a virtual event, like a special sale at your eBay Store.

Communicate on MySpace

Leaving comments. After you become someone's MySpace friend, visit their profile and add a comment. This is an effective networking tool—not only will your new friend read your comment, but people who visit your friend's page will see it, too. Avoid the most overused MySpace comment: "Thanks for the add," which is shorthand for "thanks for adding me as a friend." That's a cliché, and a missed opportunity. Take a moment to think of a meaningful comment, based on something about your new friend's profile, like, "Hey, Blade Runner is my favorite movie, too!"

- **Sending messages.** MySpace has an internal e-mail system and an instant-messaging system for sending private notes. You can include your regular e-mail signature, including links and photos. But if the message isn't too personal, you're better off posting your thoughts publicly, as a "comment" on your friend's page. This increases your visibility on MySpace, making it that much easier for new friends and readers to discover you.

- **Responding to messages.** When you receive a MySpace message, you'll receive an alert at the e-mail address you used to register at MySpace. To network effectively, respond promptly to your messages. If someone makes the effort to write to you, they'll be waiting for a response. Don't alienate potential friends by letting messages pile up unanswered.

Sending personal replies is time-consuming and you won't see instant results. But remember, the personal connection you provide with a thoughtful reply is something people will remember. These are the folks who will feel good about buying from you and recommend you to others. Marketing experts call these people "influencers" because once you've made a good impression on them, they tell their friends. This word-of-mouth process is amplified and accelerated on networks like MySpace. Connecting with these influencers is a powerful way to make your business stand out amid the clutter and noise on the Web.

- **Sending bulletins.** Once you've built a network of MySpace friends, the ability to send them MySpace bulletins is a powerful tool. Your bulletin won't be e-mailed like your personal messages are, but the headlines will appear on all your friends' "bulletin board" areas. Whether you have two dozen MySpace friends or 20,000, the ability to let them all know about a new product or offer simultaneously is a precious tool.

To post a bulletin, click the **Post bulletin** link in the box labeled **My Mail**.

Like personal messages, bulletins are a feature you'll want to use sparingly, to preserve their impact. If you bombard friends with frequent bulletins that aren't compelling, they'll start ignoring them, and they might become irritated enough to drop you as a friend.

- **Picking your 'Top 8.'** After you've explored MySpace a bit, you'll notice under each member's **About Me** section are pictures of eight friends, along with a link to that member's complete friends list. By default, the eight pictures displayed are the first eight friends added by that member, known in MySpace parlance as the Top 8.

You can shuffle your Top 8 to add zing to your profile page. Take your most influential or well-known friends and move them to the front by scrolling down to the box labeled **My Friend Space** and clicking **Change my Top Friends**.

For example, let's imagine you sell Beatles memorabilia. You'd want to send Paul McCartney an invitation and make him a Top Friend (http://myspace.com/paulmccartney).

Seek out your favorite customers or celebrities connected with your kind of merchandise, and request they add you as a friend. Move them into your Top 8, too. This is a valuable cross-promotion tool because it boosts your exposure among members who are in your target market.

If you're really popular on MySpace, don't limit yourself to just eight top friends. Click **Change my Top Friends**, and on the top left corner of the screen you'll see a drop-down menu where you can increase the number of Top Friends displayed on your main page to as many as 40. If you'd rather display fewer Top Friends, you can reduce it to four.

Work it good

After you've signed up at MySpace, pay special attention to these elements of your profile:

Headline. When you set up your MySpace account, you're able to upload a picture—perhaps your portrait or an image of your store or leading product—and a short message labeled your **headline**. Use this space to identify yourself and your business: who you are, and what you do. Use this to its maximum effect. You can update this section any time.

About Me. Here, list your history and your influences. HTML is allowed in this section, so include prominent links to your own Web site or blog if you have one.

Photos. Whether you use a photo of yourself, your company's logo or an image of a product, use professional photos and artwork when possible. Hire a real photographer or enlist a talented friend with a digital camera. Don't brand yourself an amateur by using a crummy snapshot.

Your MySpace blog. As a MySpace member you're able to publish a blog linked to your profile. Here you can include content too lengthy for your messages or bulletins. Blog posts are searchable through MySpace and regular search engines like Google, so naturally you'll want to include plenty of information about your business.

Ask your friends to "subscribe" to your blog by clicking **Subscribe to this Blog** while they're visiting. Then they'll receive e-mail alerts of your new posts.

To add a post to your blog, click **Manage Blog** from the menu just to the right of your main profile picture, then scroll down to the box labeled **My Controls** and click **Post New Blog.**

Contests and giveaways are reliable ways to promote products on MySpace too; the only limit is your imagination. You can post the details on your blog or your profile page itself. Offer a monthly drawing for a free product or service, awarded to one of your new friends. Just the act of offering a free product will encourage others to browse your wares—they won't want to wait to see if they've won the contest. However, don't go overboard with expensive prizes, and don't call what you're doing a "sweepstakes," since this is against MySpace rules.

- **MySpace groups.** Joining various MySpace "groups" is perhaps the best way to find new friends. From MySpace.com, click **Groups** on the top navigation bar. On the left, you'll see a link for **Search Groups**, where you can search for your topic area. For example, if you sell automobile accessories, you'll want to join the "MySpace Automotive Group" and the "Classic Collector and Muscle Group," among others. You can search for groups by keyword or browse by broad categories, such as "Fashion & Style" and "Pets & Animals." The groups with the most members will be listed on top. MySpace has groups specifically for eBay sellers too.

Joining groups is a better way to connect with potential customers than just randomly sending friend invitations to any profile that you happen to see. Some groups allow you to post bulletins where you can mention your business or product. But check on this: It's important to know the group's terms of use, and you don't want to be accused of spamming the group.

You can create your own MySpace group, giving members several more avenues to discover you. You can attract a wider circle of friends by forming a group dedicated to your business or product type. To create a MySpace group, from the main Groups page, click Create Group.

• **Interests.** Here's where members enter their basic likes, in categories such as books, music, movies, television, and others. Don't leave this blank. This is how many people will find you on MySpace, by searching for friends who have common interests.

• **Videos.** Video is a great way to promote yourself and your work on MySpace. People respond more when they can associate a face and a voice with the rest of your presentation.

Lots of new companies have popped up recently to provide online video content. YouTube is the most famous example, and you can also use video on eBay and blogs.

The prices of digital camcorders suitable for taking online video have fallen below $100, so it's never been easier to create your own video. A simple question-and-answer session can provide video content to publicize your business. Have a friend ask a series of questions about your business. Or, you can just describe one of your eBay items yourself.

For example, here's an archived copy of a video one eBay seller used to showcase a rare book and attract a top bid of $379:

http://provoicetracks.com/ebay/RushdieMidnightMov2.wmv

MySpace best practices

Here are several more rules of thumb for using MySpace as a publicity tool, and you can apply these same principles to most other social-networking sites:

• **It's better to give than receive.** Don't give the hard-sell. Social networking is all about communication and providing valuable information that will draw others to you. Be generous and you'll be richer.

• **Try to keep your MySpace profile streamlined and clutter-free.** Make sure that anyone who sees it can easily discover your business.

• **Focus on your target market.** Don't get sidetracked marketing to millions of people who aren't the right fit for your product or service. You'll quickly get overwhelmed, and you'll waste time communicating with people who aren't going to be interested.

• **If you're advertising a local business, be sure to include your city on your display name.** You'll improve your response because your city name will catch the eye of the people in your region.

• **Have a signup form to capture e-mail addresses.** An opt-in list of prospects will become more valuable the larger it grows. To encourage signups, offer a widget, newsletter, coupon or some other incentive.

• **Link to your own Web site.** Briefly describe the benefits visitors will find there.

• **Keep your name in front of people by posting frequently to your MySpace blog and by sending a bulletin of the blog entry to all your friends.** But don't abuse the privilege—if you post too frequently without something of value, your friends will quickly decide to ignore you, or delete you from their list of friends.

- **Don't send unsolicited messages to MySpace users.** The message will either be ignored or the user will report it as spam, perhaps prompting MySpace to disable or delete your account.

- **Don't send more than 300 friend requests in a single day.** MySpace monitors usage of your account and can restrict your privileges or even delete your account if they deem you're using it for "commercial" purposes or spam. Don't use scripts or software robots to send friend requests because this can prompt MySpace to unceremoniously delete you.

- **Don't feel obligated to accept every friend who zaps an invitation your way.** It's best to concentrate on having 50 friends you truly connect with, rather than having thousands of friends you quickly forget about.

- **To leverage MySpace as a professional asset, your page must look professional.** Your potential friends will check out your existing friends. It's fine to have some oddballs in there, but be certain you have a clear connection with your Top 8 friends.

- **To keep the hits coming, you've got to maintain your MySpace page.** Throwing together a page and never visiting or tweaking it will do little good.

- **Don't promote your MySpace profile at the expense of your own domain.** MySpace is a great networking tool, but you don't want to depend on it exclusively. If you've got your own Web site, that should be your priority, and you should use MySpace to feed traffic to your site.

Like other Web services, MySpace has a Terms of Service document that outlines what is allowed and prohibited on the site. Among other things, MySpace outlaws these activities:

- "Commercial" use of the site, such as harvesting names or contact information in order to send unsolicited commercial messages.

• Publishing physical contact information such as phone numbers, street addresses, and e-mail addresses.

• Posting content deemed offensive, illegal or that violates the rights, harms, or threatens the safety of any person.

See the full MySpace Terms of Service here:

www.myspace.com/Modules/Common/Pages/ TermsConditions.aspx

Save time on MySpace

By default, MySpace sends you e-mail notifications whenever you receive new messages, comments, blog comments, or new friend requests. Once your friend list exceeds a few hundred people, you can save time by turning off these automated alerts and simply managing your profile by logging into MySpace once a day.

To stop MySpace's automated e-mails, go to MySpace.com and click **Account Settings**. Check the box labeled "Do not send me notification emails," then click the **Change** button at the bottom of the page.

You can also save time by delegating certain MySpace administrative tasks to an assistant or colleague, such as:

• Locating potential new friends and sending invitations.

• Posting prewritten materials to your MySpace blog.

• Screening incoming friend requests and, when appropriate, approving them.

However, you should appoint a single individual within your organization to engage with the community of MySpace and other sites where you're participating. This helps ensure you project a consistent message.

- **Customizing MySpace**. Once you have mastered the basics of MySpace, you may want to further customize your profile by adjusting the background colors and text sizes and placements. You can alter the appearance of various elements of your profile by going to MySpace.com and clicking **Edit Profile**, and inserting HTML (Hyper-Text Markup Language) code into most of the portions of your profile where you've entered text. For example, to make a word in your profile appear in bold text, you'd insert the opening tag **** before the word, and after the word you'd use the closing tag, ****. Other tags can be used to change the size, color, and position of your text, or to add pictures and other graphical elements. To see a list of HTML tags, see this reference site:

www.htmlquick.com/reference/tags.html

For more ideas on customizing your profile with more elaborate layout tools, see this reference site:

www.pimp-my-profile.com

Network some more

This sector of the Internet is growing and changing at a terrific rate, and bears watching. It's entirely possible that MySpace won't continue its overwhelming domination of Internet social networking. Already, niche social networks are emerging, splintering audiences into narrower interests. Someday an entrepreneur will launch the "MySpace" of woodworking supplies, scuba gear, or auto parts. Be on the lookout for up-and-coming networks in your sphere. Or perhaps you'll have an idea for launching a network yourself.

Here are other leading social networking sites. You can navigate to each of these sites by adding a **.com** to the end of the names:

- **LinkedIn**, known as a business-to-business social network, helps professionals find and contact one another to find new jobs or leads by referral only. LinkedIn has no chat rooms or discussion boards, and personal profiles have no photos.

● **Facebook** made its name by serving college students who wanted to network with other students at their campus. More than 80 percent of students who attend U.S. colleges have a profile, according to one survey. In 2006 Facebook began accepting non-students, and now has many members from the business community, military and other sectors.

● **Gather** caters to middle-aged users, and is backed by public radio's American Public Media Group. Unlike most other networks, Gather advertises on television to lure new members, then pays members for submitting content to the site.

● **SecondLife** is a three-dimensional virtual world in which users interact with one another using avatars, an icon or representation of a member. Second Life is growing quickly and could popularize the idea of avatar-based marketing.

● **Classmates** allows members to keep in touch with high school and college classmates. Unlike most other networks, members must pay a fee to access other profiles and contact friends.

● **Flickr** is a social network for sharing photos, although photos can also be made private. Users can tag their photos with keywords, which enables others to search for them.

● **Xanga** emphasizes blogs, and allows members to enhance their profiles with special features by paying a fee.

● **Orkut**, owned by Google, has not penetrated the U.S. market yet but someday may benefit greatly from its connection to the search engine giant.

● **Bebo** is especially popular among young adults, with an average user age of about 20. Users can add home-made polls and quizzes to their profile.

● **Friendster** was one of the early popular social networking sites and has more than 30 million active users. Users create profiles and add music and video clips and blogs. The site is a little less flexible than MySpace, which overtook it in 2004 as the most popular.

• **Ning.com.** The company Ning hosts a free, easy-to-use Web platform enabling anyone to create their own social network, and more than 60,000 people have already done so. At **www.Ning.com**, you can create a customized social network by choosing a combination of features, including blogs, photos and forums. You can add your brand logo, then invite friends and customers to create their own personal profile pages on your network.

What attracts many business operators to Ning is the element of control. Unlike MySpace, where customers might be lured away by advertising for competing products and services, Ning allows the creator of a social network to administer membership, content and advertising.

Work the net

No matter which of the social networks you use, there are broad principles you can apply to each to attract attention and maximize your effectiveness.

• Include testimonials from happy customers or well-known people in your field. Anyone can have a profile on a social network, but the ones that are taken seriously have credible people vouching for their trustworthiness.

• Have the largest number of friends possible within your target market. The more complete your list, the better the odds that new people in your target market will discover you promptly.

Marketing with widgets

Most of the social-networking profiles mentioned here offer some type of "widget"—a small icon that represents a business, and links to a Web page, video or some other place online.

Widget marketing reflects the physical world, such as someone who sports a bumper sticker for his favorite radio station. But with widget marketing, the reach is wider; the cost lower. Widget marketing is effective because it's often considered to be advice from a friend, not an advertisement.

Widgets are an important tool for viral marketing on social networks and blogs.

• A Web widget is a mini tool—a chunk of code your friends can plug into their MySpace page, Web site, or blog. Widgets are usually a snippet of HTML code but can also use Adobe Flash or JavaScript programming languages. Fortunately for eBay sellers, there's a simple way to add a widget to your MySpace page (or your blog or Web site) by using the service **eBay To Go.**

Using eBay To Go, you can create a widget for a single item, multiple items (as many as 10) or a search result.

Sign up at this Web page:

http://togo.ebay.com

You'll receive a snippet of code that will place the widget on your MySpace page or blog. You can give your friends and other bloggers the same widget to display your item too. Here's an example of an eBay To Go widget:

Get your own place

Once you've started a successful eBay business, you've got the building blocks for expanding into a larger-scale operation. From there, the logical next steps are with an eBay Store and your own Web site.

Few people can benefit more from a Web site than an online seller. A simple do-it-yourself site can provide a huge visibility boost at very low cost. Even if you are active on social networking sites, it's smart to maintain a Web site or blog that serves as your online home base, a place where you have total control.

The big advantage of having your own Web site is that it enables you to sell items directly to customers without having to pay eBay selling fees. It's not going to make you rich overnight, but a Web site with moderate traffic can produce nice side income to complement your existing eBay business.

After setting up their own Web site, many sellers begin focusing on using eBay as a customer acquisition tool. They attract new customers with their exposure on eBay. Then, once they have a list of satisfied customers, they market to them periodically via e-mail, the Web and blogs.

Several vendors have prepackaged solutions that enable sellers to quickly open a store on their own Web site. By keeping customers at their own Web sites, sellers can potentially avoid hefty selling fees and losing sales to competitors offering the same item on eBay for a few cents less.

Vendio is an example of one vendor who can host your store on the Internet:

http://www.vendio.com/services/stores.html

• **eBay ProStores.** eBay also offers independent merchants a store hosting solution through its ProStores unit, which serves small- and medium-sized businesses. ProStores provides a customizable online storefront, allowing you to use your own Web address instead of your eBay URL. ProStores provides domain registration and hosting, a shopping cart function, and credit card processing. Three levels of service are offered, with fees ranging from $29.95 to $249.95 per month. For more information, see:

http://www.prostores.com/

Here are examples of two stores hosted by ProStores:

http://www.bustedknucklegarage.com/

http://www.beadforlife.org/

There is lots of competition in the store-hosting field, but don't skimp and go with a fly-by-night provider just to save a few dollars. The danger is that if your vendor fails or goes out of business, your business can go down the tubes with it. If you have a Web-based store, your site can go down when your vendor's computers crash. And if the vendor goes out of business, your store might be lost for good.

Another problem with having your own Web store is you need to attract customers. It's not like eBay, where buyers have already con- gregated. Buyers won't find your site unless you market it somehow. In addition to promoting your store on MySpace and blogs, e-mail can be an effective marketing tool. Be sure to provide a way for recipients to opt out of receiving your e-mails, however. You don't want to be accused of sending spam. If you market your Web site with unsolicited e-mails, you're required to comply with the CAN-SPAM Act. The law requires advertising e-mails sent to someone you don't have an existing business relationship with to:

- Be identified as an advertisement.

- Have a valid return e-mail address.

- Have a legitimate subject heading.

- Include an opt-out or unsubscribe provision.

- Include your physical mailing address.

Get involved

Many sellers outsource their Web project to someone they've found in the local Yellow Pages, paying a designer $500 or more to build what amounts to an online brochure. That's a big mistake, because static Web sites with little content don't draw the repeat traffic that will bring you new business.

Although it may seem like a daunting technical challenge at first, building your own site is easier than ever, thanks to improved software tools. Every major Internet hosting company now offers a variety of design templates you can use to start quickly, without having to learn computer coding. You'll gain much more from your Web site if it's maintained by you or a close associate.

Two basic options exist for those establishing their first site:

- **Do it yourself** by registering a domain name and building your own site. This option requires you to learn a few software tools, but provides more flexibility and control. **GoDaddy.com** offers fast, reliable service, and a wide variety of Web domain registration and hosting plans at competitive prices. There's no setup fee and no annual commitment is required. GoDaddy's economy plan includes 5 giga-bytes of disk space, 500 e-mail accounts, forums, blogging, and photo galleries for $3.99 a month. This hosting company and most competitors such as **www.Register.com** offer simple tools and templates for building your own site.

- **Using a free account** at a network such as MySpace.com, Google Pages, Blogger.com, or LiveJournal.com. A packaged solution like this is easy to learn, but provides less flexibility. Some sites feature advertising you can't control, which can distract visitors from your message.

One way to get started quickly while preserving your future options is to pay GoDaddy or another registrar $9 to register your own domain name, such as **www.YourName.com**, then forwarding the traffic to your account at eBay, MySpace, Blogger, or wherever you wish. Later, when you have time to build a dedicated site, you can forward the traffic there. This strategy allows you to start building your online traffic now without the risk of losing regular traffic if you switch your focus to another site.

In any case, it's prudent to make backup copies of all content you post to a free account on sites like Blogger or MySpace, since these free accounts are sometimes deleted accidentally.

For the past several years, Web hosting providers have consistently lowered their prices and added features to stay competitive. For example, one of the leading do-it-yourself Web store services, City-Max.com, lets you create a site in five minutes, including a credit-card processing account with no setup fee, integration with PayPal, and an interface for easy eBay auction listing. Fees start at $19.98 a month, which includes an e-mail account and free domain name registration.

Master your domain

If you're committed to actively supporting your business online, it's best to stake out your own territory on the Web. This means registering your own domain name, which you alone control. GoDaddy.com, Register.com and NetworkSolutions.com are well known, reliable firms where you can buy a package of services—domain registration, Web hosting and e-mail accounts.

You may want to use the name of your business as the domain. Or you may want to use the name of a product, registering a domain for each product. Keep your domain name short and memorable so people who see it or hear of it can recall it. Hyphenated domain names are usually a bad idea—they're harder to remember and they fail the "radio test" because they're difficult to repeat in conversation.

Build blocks

The great thing about a Web site is you can always add to it. Here are some basic elements you'll want to consider adding to your site:

- Content. Nobody will visit a site that's merely an advertisement. Your content can be a series of articles or even feedback from your customers.

- Your biography.

- Links to purchase your products, either on your site, eBay or elsewhere. The more choices you offer buyers, the better.

- Reviews of your products or services.

- A form where visitors can enter their e-mail address to subscribe to a newsletter or site updates.

- Contact information—your e-mail address (or a form that forwards messages) and perhaps postal address and phone number.

Part of creating a useful, valuable Web site is understanding the behavior of your visitors—how they find your site, and what they do once they arrive. Depending on which Web host you've selected, you'll have access to some type of traffic reports that can provide valuable insight into which of your content pages are most effective.

If you're doing any paid advertising, these reports can also help you figure out whether your ads are effective. Google Analytics is a very good free tool that provides detailed statistics about the activity of your visitors, and it's fairly easy to add the service to your site. For more information:

www.Google.com/Analytics

- **Linking strategy.** Many bloggers publish a list of links to related blogs on their sidebar, known as a *blogroll*. This can be helpful for your visitors, but it can be overdone. You should strike a balance between giving your visitors easy access to useful, outside information, while not encouraging them to leave your site sooner than they otherwise might.

It's counterproductive to link to marginally related sites from your home page because it dilutes your site's "authority" in Google rankings. A better solution is to link to outside content from within individual blog posts when relevant. Build a separate "resources" page on your site where you can point visitors to outside resources without getting penalized on your home page.

Bait search engines

The beauty of publishing a blog is that it naturally optimizes your content for indexing by search engines. A blog makes you highly visible, without your having to think too much about technique. Even so, it helps to know some basics of search engine optimization (SEO) to enhance your site's ability to draw new visitors.

The leading search engines are Google, Yahoo, and MSN.com. If your site doesn't already appear in search results, request that your site be added. To request indexing by the search engines, go to:

- Google:**http://Google.com/addurl.html**

- MSN: **http://Search.MSN.com/docs/submit.aspx**

- Yahoo: **http://Search.Yahoo.com/info/submit.html**

Another way to get your site included in the search engines is to have at least one incoming link from another site that's already been indexed by search engines. The next time Google and other search engines crawl the other site, they'll follow the link to yours.

The essential ingredients for a high-ranking site change periodically. Many bloggers and Webmasters waste time and money chasing the "perfect" formula for getting to the top of search results, and then must start over when Google changes the way it evaluates Web pages. Rather than spending lots of time trying to game the system, you can better spend your time adding valuable content to your site.

Be dense

One way to make your content more visible with search engines is *keyword density.* Let's imagine you're writing a blog post (or an article on your Web site) about how to wax a car with a buffer you sell. You might write the title: "Wax your car in 10 minutes with a buffer: Here's how." This way, the most important words, *wax, car,* and *buffer* appear at the beginning of your title. Your first sentence might be, "Waxing your car can be a time-consuming chore, but here's how to get it done fast." This reinforces your keywords. Repeating them again will enhance your keyword density and ensure your post ranks high in searches for those keywords.

Be consistent with word choices to maintain keyword density. Let's imagine you have a page on your site devoted to antique Ford Thunderbird cars. Naturally, you'll want *Thunderbird* to appear several times on the page to rank high in search results for that keyword. So you'll want to keep using the word *Thunderbird* instead of slang or nicknames. The sentence "The 1969 *'Bird* was a stylish car" would dilute your keyword density.

Although keyword density makes it easier for your target audience to find you, don't overdo it. If you artificially jam the same keyword several times in each sentence, search engines will detect this and penalize you for "keyword stuffing."

Another way to get penalized with search engines is by participating in so-called "link farms." These are sites that trade or sell Web links, but it seldom works. The only links that will truly boost your site are from high-ranking sites with content similar to yours. So forget about buying links to boost your SEO. Simply produce good content for your audience, and the links and traffic will come naturally.

You've probably seen advertisements for consultants who promise to make your site No. 1 in the search engines within 30 days. Don't waste your money. Chances are, anyone who makes such promises can't deliver.

Your most important links will be from stand-alone sites in your niche. Links from crowded social sites like MySpace or discussion boards won't strengthen your site's rankings much, says Dave Taylor, author of *Growing Your Business with Google*. "Theoretically all links are good, but I don't believe that links from jungles like MySpace are going to give you any real boost," Taylor says. Google provides a tutorial for optimizing your site:

www.Google.com/Support/Webmasters

Lengthen your lease

Many factors influencing how much juice your Web site has are outside your immediate control. For example, if your domain is new—registered within the previous year—it will get short shrift in search results. Some experts call this the *Google sandbox effect*, meaning that new Web sites are given a probationary period.

Why would Google penalize new blogs and Web sites? Isn't a new blogger or Webmaster just as capable of producing valuable content? The answer is, newcomers are penalized to help the search engines deal with spam Web sites, a growing problem. Fly-by-night companies build spam sites using stolen content or machine-generated lists of keywords. The spammers sprinkle their sites with Google advertising and make a bit of money, at least until Google wises up and cuts off its ads. To limit their costs, the spammers register their domain for the minimum, one year—they don't want to pay in advance for a site they'll be abandoning soon. Google limits the traffic it sends to new sites to avoid helping these spammers make even more money.

How can you turn this to your advantage? By letting Google and the other search engines know your site isn't spam. Extend your domain registration several years into the future, instead of paying the one-year minimum. By paying your domain registration fees nine years in advance, you'll spend about $90 instead of the minimum $9 for one year. But the $90 investment can provide a big return. Bloggers and Webmasters report huge increases in search-engine traffic just weeks after extending their domain registration for multiple years, according to anecdotal reports.

- **Privacy policies.** If you collect data from your Web site visitors, consider posting a disclaimer. Privacy policies explain how names, addresses, and other information are used or shared with third parties.

    The Better Business Bureau provides this suggested outline for privacy policies:

www.bbbonline.org/privacy/sample_privacy.asp

Wait for results

Building a Web site can be a lonely process. Don't expect a big response in the first month or even the next six months. Often it takes an entire year for a Web site or blog to gain momentum. But if you concentrate on producing a useful site with quality content, word will get around.

As you build your site, keep one general idea in mind: Unless you're already a superstar or your business is well known, don't make your Web site about *you*. Make it about *your visitor*. Provide compelling content that solves problems, entertains, sparks curiosity, or inspires. Everything else will follow.

Resist the temptation to pack your site with fancy features like flashy graphics or voices or music that plays automatically. Usually these doodads have the opposite effect than what was intended—they make your site slow, irritating, noisy and hard to read.

Earn side revenue

Steady traffic on your Web site provides additional income opportunities through affiliate programs and advertising. If your site becomes extremely popular, the revenue could be substantial.

Some bloggers report that a combination of affiliate and advertising revenue can result in about 1.5 cents of income for each unique daily visitor to your site. At that rate, a site averaging 1,500 unique daily visitors can generate about $8,200 in annual revenue—not bad for something that requires no ongoing work on your part. Depending on your audience and the type of products related to your niche, you might do better or worse.

New sites usually generate negligible revenue, but advertising or affiliate programs can still be worthwhile. Your audience may appreciate niche advertising, and these programs can boost your visibility with search engines. One option is to donate your affiliate and ad revenues to charities admired by your audience, which sometimes can be handled automatically. The public-relations benefit of donating could outweigh the monetary value, and you won't have to account for it as income and pay tax on it.

In any case, advertising shouldn't overly distract visitors from the main purpose of your site—generating awareness of your business. Here are some of the leading advertising and affiliate programs you can use on your Web site:

- **Commission Junction.** Opening an account at Commission Junction provides access to hundreds of niche affiliate programs. You'll find affiliate opportunities for nearly any type of product, including dozens of specialized retailers. The site provides the codes you'll need to insert on your Web site, and consolidated reports of your commissions.

www.CommissionJunction.com

eBay. If there's a category of merchandise on eBay of interest to your target market, open an affiliate account. You can display relevant ads for popular auctions on your site. According to eBay, its top 25 affiliates average more than $100,000 in commissions every month.

The ads contain product information, gallery images, bidding prices, and ending times. eBay claims that the click-through rates for these ads are double that of regular banner ads.

eBay sellers may earn commissions from sending traffic to their own listings or to listings of other sellers. Using eBay's affiliate Editor's Kit, sellers can display their own listings on a Web site or blog, and they can cross-promote items from other sellers and earn commissions on all resulting sales. However, eBay doesn't allow sellers to use affiliate links on eBay pages such as View Item pages, My eBay or My World.

After joining, you can operate your eBay affiliate account through the Commission Junction service, mentioned above.

For more information, see:

http://affiliates.ebay.com

- **Amazon Associates.** Amazon's affiliate program is called Amazon Associates. You can display links for your product and related ones on Amazon. When your visitors click through to Amazon and make a purchase, you're paid a commission. Typically your commission is a few percentage points of the total sale, depending on the type of merchandise.

Amazon Associates is one of the most familiar and successful programs on the Internet, with more than 1 million member sites. After joining you receive an Associates ID code, which you insert into your links to Amazon products.

After your visitors click on your Associates link, you'll receive commissions on most other purchases those customers make during the following 24 hours. For example, if your visitor buys a plasma TV on Amazon during that same 24-hour session, you'll get a commission on that too.

In 2006 Amazon Associates introduced a contextual program called Omakase, which displays different products based on the content on your site and your visitor's browsing history at Amazon. The advantage for affiliates is that Omakase is dynamic, exposing your audience to different products each time they visit a different page on your site, increasing the odds of a purchase.

The name Omakase is Japanese for "Leave it up to us," a custom in Japanese restaurants in which the chef improvises a meal based on his knowledge of the diner's preferences.

For more information, visit:

www.Amazon.com/Associates

• **Google AdSense.** Google's AdSense program is perhaps the best-known Web ad network, and it's relatively easy to sign up and incorporate text or banner ads onto your site. For more information, see:

www.Google.com/Adsense

Two alternatives to AdSense are **www.AdBrite.com** and **www.BlogAds.com**.

Use social search

In the mid 1990s, Yahoo, the first popular Web portal, guided most Internet traffic with a simple hand-picked menu of sites. Yahoo's editors decided which Web sites were worth pointing to, and that's where the traffic went. At the time, it seemed like a good system, and much more efficient than search engines, which tended to spit out mountains of irrelevant results. Back then, it sometimes seemed easier to find a needle in a haystack than to find anything with a search engine.

Then Google built a better mousetrap. Instead of relying on humans to figure out which content is best, Google's computers determined relevance and authority. Google's PageRank system considers not only the words contained on a Web page, but also how many related sites link in. Each incoming link is a vote on a page's importance, helping it rise to the top of Google's search results.

As good as Google's system is, however, it can't always deliver relevant results, particularly for specialized content. Sometimes providing good search results requires direct human brainpower, something provided by *social search* tools. Social search works best in deep niches, where people who truly understand the content render judgments. In these cases, social search can be more accurate than Google's algorithmic search, which counts links only.

Why should you care about social search? Because more and more people are using it to find information about things they want to buy.

Here's what can happen if your blog or Web site is mentioned favorably on a social search service—a flood of 5,000 to 10,000 visitors can visit within hours. This crowd can include thousands of folks highly passionate about what you're selling, including those nearly impossible to reach through traditional advertising or publicity.

Dozens of popular sites have emerged in the past few years providing tools for search, social networking, and social bookmarking:

- **http://del.icio.us** was launched in 2004 and is a dominant social bookmarking site. It's a handy way for people to store their favorite Web bookmarks online where they're portable, instead of on the PC, confined to one machine.

For example, someone shopping for a new stereo might compile product reviews on his Delicious account while deciding which one to buy. Instead of having a hard-to-read list of bookmarks in a drop-down menu on their Web browser, users just consult their del.icio.us page to view their favorite Web resources, along with their own annotations.

To organize their bookmarks, del.icio.us users use tags, making it easy for other del.icio.us users to find that same content. That's the real value of social bookmarking: the ability to share bookmarks with others, instantly tapping into collective wisdom.

For example, let's imagine you want to buy exotic tropical fish. From the del.icio.us home page, you search for "tropical fish." Instead of finding only the most *universally popular* sites Google shows you, on del.icio.us you find the *favorite* resources of tropical-fish fanatics. These are the resources valued by the people with experience, the people who eat, breathe and sleep tropical fish.

Shared resources are the ones with real word of mouth, not just a certain number of links or brute-force advertising. The results are the best in the judgment of those who know the most. There's no substitute for recommendations by people who've consumed the content and found it important, useful or entertaining.

Search is what you do when you know what you're looking for. *Discovery* is how you find what you didn't know existed.

If you're using Web content to help drive traffic to your eBay business, your goal is to work your way into people's bookmarks on del.icio.us and similar bookmarking sites. How do you do it? By having articles that are really, really interesting and helpful to people who care about that topic.

- **Smart crowds.** When del.icio.us users save a Web page as a bookmark, they're "voting" for the page, much as Google ranks measure how popular a page is by counting incoming links. But with social bookmarks, individuals vote. With social sites, everyone votes, not just Webmasters and bloggers. Since individual Internet users vastly outnumber Webmasters or bloggers, the collective wisdom is much richer.

Once someone mentions you on del.icio.us—by bookmarking your blog or Web site—it's much easier for people to find you, and you'll get a new stream of people coming to your site who are already interested in what you have to say.

You can hope that people will take it on themselves to bookmark you on del.icio.us, or you can make it easy for them. You can configure your blog or Web store to automatically insert a small **add to del.icio.us** button to the bottom of all your content. Every reader who clicks the button casts another vote for you. For instructions on adding these buttons, see:

www.publisher.yahoo.com/social_media_tools

Get vertical

Another example of a social search tool is a *Swicki*, which improves and personalizes its results based on feedback from your site's users.

By installing a Swicki on your site, users can customize their search results. They can vote up the relevant results they see, and vote down the irrelevant results. The search engine learns from its users.

Swicki is a play on the words search and wiki, implying that its value comes from user input. The tool is provided free by a company called Eurekster. It can also produce some additional income for your site, if you elect to show the paid ads Swickis offers. For more information, see:

www.Swicki.com

Google is getting into the personalized-search field, too. In 2006 it began testing Google Customized Search, which is linked to its AdSense program. You can specify the Web sites you want searched and integrate its search box and results into your own site. See:

www.Google.com/coop/cse

www.Digg.com is a news community run by amateur news buffs instead of professional news editors. Members submit items of note they've found somewhere on the Web and vote for the ones they like. A typical entry might read: "A Windmill for Your Backyard? A new, affordable wind turbine promises to help homeowners fight rising energy costs." Readers would click through to the site or blog, read the original article, then vote it up (digg it) or down (undigg).

If your blog or Web site gets voted up on Digg, you can expect a crush of visitors within minutes

Got a killer auction? Nominate it on Digg.com and get thousands of hits.

Originally Digg was narrowly focused on technology news, but in 2006 it expanded into a broader array of topics. One of the most popular categories is dedicated to great deals on products found anywhere on the Web. If an item (a link to a Web page) receives enough votes, it's promoted to Digg's home page, where it's often read by hundreds of thousands of members who often click through to the blog or Web site for further information, or perhaps blog about it themselves.

www.Flickr.com is a social bookmarking site focusing solely on photographs. Amateur and professional photographers upload their favorite photos to share with friends and strangers, who can assign tags and add comments. Yahoo bought Flickr in 2005.

Get more free advertising

Most people don't purchase something the first time they hear of it. It can take six or seven exposures to prompt a consumer to buy. The more frequently you can pop up in front of your potential audience—providing valuable, free content—the larger your audience becomes. When Internet searchers discover valuable content, they become prime candidates for buying an item or ordering a service from someone regarded as an expert.

The benefits of posting free sample content online grow by the day. Not only can consumers find you, but reporters and news producers increasingly turn to the Internet to find expert sources and story ideas. This can lead to exposure and credibility that can't be bought at any price.

Here are some good ways of providing sample content to burnish your reputation and achieve expert status. In some cases, your friends and customers even create this content for you:

- **Post question-and-answer content.** On your blog or Web site, summarize the best questions you receive from customers via e-mail, phone calls, letters or personal conversations. Publish them in a question-and-answer format. This provides interesting, valuable and easy-to-read content. Q&A content is simple to produce, especially if you're already producing the raw material by answering e-mails. When you post this content publicly, your entire audience benefits, instead of just one person (although you should omit personally identifying information where appropriate). Further, Q&As expand your audience because the format boosts your visibility with search engines. Many people searching the Web actually type questions or sentence fragments into Google, such as "How to restore old photographs." You can rewrite the questions for clarity, or even write the question yourself to help illustrate a point. You can use this same type of content to build an FAQ, or Frequently Asked Questions, page on your site.

- **Participate in online discussions.** Answering queries about your favorite topics on discussion boards and e-mail lists can lure more visitors to your Web site or eBay Store. Find relevant groups on Web boards and in groups sponsored by Yahoo, MSN, LiveJournal and America Online. Add a three- or four-line signature to the bottom of your posts, including your seller name and URL. Be sure to provide helpful information; don't post purely promotional messages. Follow the rules of the group, which sometimes preclude commercial content.

- **Post comments on blogs related to your topic.** Most blogs allow you to include a link back to your site in your comment. Invest the time in providing useful, thoughtful commentary, and you'll bring some new visitors to your site.

Bank articles

An increasingly popular way to get free exposure is by contributing to online article banks. One of the most popular, **EzineArticles.com**, has more than 55,000 members who post content. Contributors aren't paid, but they figure the added exposure is worth the effort.

If your articles are accepted, they're featured on EzineArticles.com and made available for reuse on other Web sites, blogs and e-mail newsletters. Each article includes a "resource box" with links back to your site.

Although article syndication can provide great exposure, be selective about the content you contribute. Don't offer any content that appears on your site without first rewriting it. Search engines such as Google filter out "duplicate content" from search results. If an article from your site appears elsewhere on the Internet, one of the Web pages probably will be deleted from search results, and chances are it will be yours. Search-engine experts call this the *duplicate content penalty*.

Avoid backfires

Let's imagine you sell pottery, and to help promote the business, you publish a pottery blog. Last year on your blog, you wrote a nifty tutorial on fixing broken pottery. Word has gotten around, and now every pottery site on the Internet links to your pottery-repair page. Because of all these links, your page is the top Google result for "repairing pottery," "fixing pottery," and several related queries. That single page is your Web site's crown jewel, accounting for half your new visitors and a good portion of your business.

Now let's imagine you try to squeeze even *more* traffic from your pottery-repair article. You post it to EzineArticles.com, without changing much except to add the links back to your site. Meanwhile, you upload the same article to other syndication sites like GoArticles.com and IdeaMarketers.com.

Now you sit back and wait for the extra traffic, but the exact opposite happens—you see less traffic, not more. Now that your article appears on a bigger, more popular site, it's likely that Google will send searchers there instead of sending them to your site. Google has made a quick calculation of which site is more authoritative, and because EzineArticles.com has more links than your site, it wins. Google doesn't care that you wrote the article and have the Internet's best pottery site.

The lesson is, keep your most valuable content on your site exclusively. And if you're going to syndicate existing content, rewrite it substantially so the search engines don't penalize you for it.

Google's Adam Lasnik, the company's "search evangelist," offers two tips for avoiding the duplicate content penalty:

- If you syndicate an article containing the same or very similar language that appears somewhere on your site, ensure the syndicated article includes a link back to the original article on your site. Don't include only a link to your home page or some other page.

- Minimize boilerplate language on all your content. For example, instead of including lengthy copyright notices at the bottom of all your Web pages, include a brief summary with a link to a page containing your full copyright notice.

None of these safeguards, however, is foolproof. The only sure way to avoid the duplicate content penalty is by syndicating original material only, and keeping your best material exclusive to your site.

Get really simple

RSS, or Really Simple Syndication, is a Web feed that allows people to view summaries of your blog posts. Readers are automatically notified when you post new material. Most blogging software automatically publishes an RSS feed for you, or you can open a free account with Feedburner, which will publish an RSS feed for you with several enhancements:

www.Feedburner.com

Although an RSS feed makes your blog more visible, there are also a few disadvantages. For example, readers who can view all your blog content within an RSS reader may quit visiting your Web site, and won't be exposed to other types of content. You can minimize this problem by syndicating a brief summary of your blog posts, perhaps the first 100 words. Readers who want to continue would need to click through to your site.

Once you're proficient with RSS, you can subscribe to feeds of a variety of information on eBay such as bulletins, discussion boards and search results. For more information:

http://pages.ebay.com/help/welcome/contextual/rss.html

Protect your content

The Internet is a great publicity vehicle because it makes your content freely available. By the same token, the openness of the Web makes it easy for people to steal your work. An unscrupulous blogger or Webmaster can copy and paste your most valuable material onto his site within minutes without asking permission.

Every month or so, you should search the Web for some of the text from several of your pages. A Google search for a string of six to eight words within quotation marks should turn up any sites that have copied your content.

A stern message to the owner of the site—or, failing that, the company that hosts the site—usually results in deletion of the stolen material. Here's an example of a cease-and-desist notice you can send via e-mail:

Dear John Doe,

It's come to my attention that you are republishing my original content from MySite.com on your Web site, YourSite.com. For example, page [ADDRESS] on your site includes the following paragraphs: [TEXT].

Your unauthorized use of my original material violates U.S. and international copyright laws. If the offending material remains available on your site 72 hours from now, I will have no choice but to pursue legal action against you.

Please comply with my request, so that we can remedy this situation without unnecessary difficulty.

Sincerely,

Jane Doe
MySite.com

If no contact information appears on the offending Web site, enter the site's domain name in the search box at:

www.Register.com/retail/whois.rcmx

This will return the name and contact information of the person or company who registered the domain or the site's hosting company. Also try sending your message to webmaster@[domain name] and abuse@[domain name].

Another source of contact information for Web sites is:

www.DomainTools.com

Blog for business

Blogging is a relatively easy way for you to publicize your business and even improve your writing while you're at it. If you can write an e-mail, you can write a blog—it's the easiest, cheapest, and perhaps best way for authors to find an audience and connect with customers. Blogging is an informal, intimate form of communication that inspires trust among your readers.

You can view the official eBay company blog here:

http://www.ebaychatter.com

For the same reasons that traditional advertising is less effective than ever, a blog can be highly effective for promoting your business. People interested in the things you sell seek out your message.

You can start an eBay blog to share your views with other eBay buyers and sellers. You can use it to enhance your eBay Store and talk about your selling activities on eBay.

To create an eBay blog:

- Go to **http://blogs.ebay.com** and click **Start Blogging.**
- Enter your name and a brief description of your blog in the blanks.

- Enter "tags" or descriptive keywords related to your blog so readers can find it by searching.

- Select a visual theme for your blog from the pre-formatted choices.

- **eBay Community Content rules.** On your eBay blog and all other areas where you can upload written material (reviews, guides, wikis, message boards, descriptions), you must adhere to eBay's Community Content rules. The rules prohibit the following:

  - Advertising off-eBay transactions.

  - Using text or images you have copied from other sources without permission.

  - Material of an adult, offensive or hateful nature.

  - Promoting giveaways or lotteries.

For more details, consult eBay's Web site:

http://pages.ebay.com/help/policies/member-created-content-ov.html

Discover blogs

Put simply, a blog is a Web site (or part of a Web site) with a few interactive features. You don't have to call it a blog unless you want to. It's possible that within a few years, nearly every Web page will have interactive features, and people simply won't call them blogs anymore.

You needn't know anything about computers to blog. Simply type into a form, and presto—the whole world can see it. Your blog is a *content management* system—a painless way to build and maintain a platform where readers can discover and enjoy your writing.

A blog can be a part of your Web site, or it can be *the* Web site. And, of course, you can have a blog on eBay, MySpace, or any number of sites.

The main thing that distinguishes a blog from a plain old Web site is that a blog is frequently updated with short messages, or *posts*. Readers often chime in with their own comments at the bottom of each post. This free exchange of ideas is what makes blogs a revolutionary tool for entrepreneurs: A successful blog is a constant stream of ideas, inspiration, perspective, and advice—it's a real-time, global focus group.

Some sellers resist the idea of blogging and the "extra work" it entails. Their reasoning is, "Why create more work?" Well, blogging can help you maximize the effectiveness of things you're probably already doing, like answering e-mails from your buyers.

Compared with other types of Internet publicity content such as static Web sites or e-mail newsletters, blogs provide three big advantages:

- Blogs are easy to start and maintain.

- The short, serialized content of blogs encourages regular readership and repeated exposure to your products or services.

- Blogs rank high in search-engine results from Google and other providers, making them easy to find.

Why do blogs get so much traffic from search engines? First, blogs are topical. When you're writing about the same topics and ideas day in and day out, your site becomes packed with the keywords your target market is searching for. Stay at it awhile, and it becomes nearly impossible for your likely customers to miss you, thanks to Google and the other search engines. Most new visitors will find your site by using a search engine, after looking for words and topics contained in your Web pages.

Another reason blogs are so easy to find is that search engines usually rank them higher than other types of Web sites. Thus your links can show up at the top of search results, which is where most people click.

Google and the other search engines give extra credit to blogs for a couple of reasons:

- Blogs are updated frequently, and the assumption is "fresh" content is more valuable.

- Blogs tend to have many links from other Web pages with similar content. The assumption is that because other bloggers and Webmasters have decided to link to your content, it's probably valuable.

Your visibility in search results is key, since about 40 percent of your new visitors will likely arrive via a Web search. If your site ranks highly in Web searches for the keywords related to your items, you'll have a constant source of well-qualified visitors and new customers.

Breathe the blogosphere

Step 1 in becoming a blogger is to consume some blogs yourself. Reading other blogs gives you a quick feel for what works, what doesn't, and the techniques you'll want to apply to your own blog.

There are millions of blogs, and finding ones that suit you can be like searching for a needle in a haystack. There's no easy way to filter out low-quality blogs—you've just got to sample what's out there.

A good place to begin is by browsing for blogs about your hobbies, pastimes and passions. You can find a list of the most popular blogs here:

www.Technorati.com/pop/blogs

You can drill down into niche territory by browsing **www.Technorati.com/blogs**, where you'll find a menu of subjects on the left. You can also search blogs by keyword at these sites:

www.Blogsearch.Google.com
www.Feedster.com
www.IceRocket.com

Once you've found a few blogs of interest, it's easy to find more. Bloggers tend to link to one another, both within their blog posts, and often within a side menu of links known as a *blogroll*.

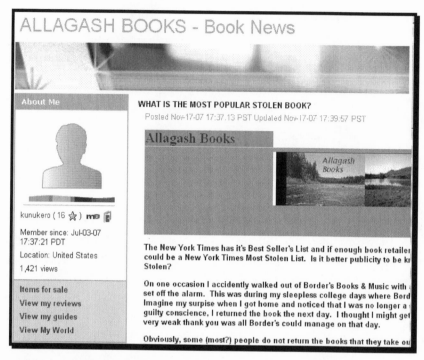

Here's an imaginative eBay blog by a member who sells used books. In this widely read post, he ponders: Which books are so treasured that they're frequently stolen?

A handy tool for keeping track of all your blogs is a *newsreader* or *aggregator*, which saves you the trouble of poking around the Web, looking for new blog posts. Instead, your newsreader gathers and displays updates for you. One free, easy-to-use reader is:

www.Bloglines.com

You'll quickly learn which blogs you've subscribed to are must-reads, and which can be ignored or deleted.

Connect with readers

It's natural to be apprehensive about starting a blog. When you first begin, it may feel like being on stage without a script or a view of the audience. Don't worry, feedback will come soon enough. Remember, there's no right or wrong way to blog. The only rule is your target audience must find something worthwhile.

It couldn't be easier to start a blog on eBay. Go to:

http://blogs.ebay.com

In the left column, follow the directions under **Get Started.**

Many other free services will host your blog. One way to ease into blogging is to start with a temporary blog at **www.Blogger.com**, where you can set up a free practice blog in five minutes. Take a dry run for a week or two, then make your blog public when you're ready.

A lively blog is like a free focus group: It provides you with constant feedback, criticism and new ideas. Your blog readers will pepper you with comments and e-mails.

Indeed, the true power of blogging is the momentum created by your audience. Once your blog has 100 frequent readers, it has critical mass. It may take six months or a year to get there, but from there it's all downhill. Members of your core audience begin competing to hand you the most useful, compelling ideas by writing comments on your blog and e-mailing you directly. That's when your blog becomes electric, a magnet attracting new visitors. Your core audience swells as word of mouth goes viral.

Value input

Most blogs include space below the author's posts for readers to add their own views. These comments can take the conversation in a totally new direction and become the most interesting material on your blog, thanks purely to your readers' efforts.

For the blogger, comments bring three key benefits:

- Instant feedback on your content, and a sense of what your audience finds valuable.

- Feeling of participation and loyalty among your audience.

- Adding valuable keyword density to your site, making it much more visible in search-engine results.

Like any tool, however, comments can be abused. It's not unusual to see rude or off-topic comments on some blogs, and even "spam comments" written solely to plant links back to the spammer's site. The worst spammers even use software robots, which scour the Web for target blogs and insert their junk links. Spam comments are usually along the lines of, "Hey, great blog. Come see us at **www.Cheap-Viagra.com**."

Fortunately, most problem comments can be prevented by using countermeasures like *comment moderation*: you review and approve new comments before they appear on your blog. Another option is to allow readers to post comments immediately, and you review them later. The advantage is your readers get immediate gratification in seeing their comments posted as they submit them.

Most spam comments can be prevented by using *word verification*, requiring comment writers to type a short series of characters displayed in an image. This stops spam comments from software robots. The technical term is CAPTCHA, which stands for "Completely Automated Public Turing test to tell Computers and Humans Apart."

Get style

Just as every business is unique, there's an endless variety of blog styles and flavors. All the blogging services have page templates, allowing you to start with a basic design and add a few personal elements.

Don't get bogged down looking for the "perfect" design. You'll always be free to tweak your design later, or do a complete overhaul. The most important thing is to get started adding content and building your audience.

The main design requirement is readability. Plain vanilla blogs are fine, and are actually preferred by most readers—it's the words that count. Black text on a white background might seem uninspired, but it's much easier on the eyes than white text on a black background or some other color. A plain masthead, simply your blog title in capital letters, is fine to start. The important thing is to get started.

Get raw material

A free, easy way to find new raw material for your blog is to create a *Google Alert*, which will automatically scour thousands of media sources for any keywords you specify. Are you a seller of collectible coffee mugs? Simply search for "mugs" and you'll be alerted via e-mail when something containing your keywords appears in newspapers, magazines, Web sites, or other sources. Sign up at:

www.Google.com/alerts

Google Alerts are also a handy way to monitor mentions of your blog title, your name, seller ID, and your competitors.

Name your blog

A blog title usually spans the top portion of each page like a newspaper masthead. Titles are usually short and catchy—perhaps just a couple of nonsense words like *Boing Boing*, or a made-up compound word like *RocketBoom* or *BuzzMachine*. The name could be a non sequitur or double-entendre like PostSecret. Sometimes a title is just a title, like *The Official Google Weblog*.

Try to include in your title the most critical keyword related to your niche. *Joe's Guide to Antique Clocks and Watches* is a good title. A poor title would be *Joe's Stitch in Time* because nobody would search for those words, and if they ran across them, couldn't guess what it's about. Be obvious. Pick a few words that will be easy for people to remember and to repeat in conversation and e-mails.

Write your posts

The essential ingredient of a blog is its short entries, or posts. They're arranged in reverse chronological order, with the newest at top. Posts can be a few sentences long, or many paragraphs long, and often link to outside information like blogs, newspaper stories, or multimedia clips hosted elsewhere on the Web.

Nearly any tidbit of information relevant to your audience can be spun into a blog post of some type:

• **Informational.** A news-oriented blurb. A new development.

• **Question/Answer.** Easy to write, and fun to read. Reliable material, even if you have to make up the question.

• **Instructional.** Can be a longer post, a tutorial that explains how to do something related to your niche.

• **Link posts.** Find an interesting blog post elsewhere. Link to it and add your own spin.

• **Rant.** Let off some steam, and let it rip. Interesting blogs don't play it safe, they take sides.

• **Book review.** Review a book related to your field. It can be a new book or a classic that newcomers haven't heard of.

• **Product reviews.** The word "review" is a popular search term. Give your frank opinion, and encourage your readers to chime in with their own views.

• **Lists.** Write about the "Top 5 Ways" to do a task, or the "Top 10 Reasons" for such-and-such. Readers love lists. If someone else publishes a list, you can summarize it or critique it on your own blog.

- **Interviews.** Chat with someone in your field. Provide a text summary on your blog. You can also add a transcript or even an audio file.

- **Case studies.** Report on how so-and-so does such-and-such. You don't have to call it a "case study," just tell the story.

- **Profiles.** Profiles focus on a particular person, a personality. The person profiled can be someone well known in your field, or perhaps a newcomer nobody's heard of.

Most blogs are conversational and informal, but that doesn't provide a license to be sloppy. You want your blog to reflect favorably on your business, and that requires attention to detail—not to mention beginning your sentences with capital letters and ending them with periods. It's worth proofreading and spell-checking your posts before publishing. Keeping your paragraphs short will minimize your rewriting chores.

One helpful feature for you and your readers is blog categories. Assign each post to one or more categories, such as "technology," "marketing," "features," "reviews," or however you can best divide your material. Category headings can be listed on your blog's margin, and are especially valuable for new readers.

Make the long haul

Blogs evolve, and priorities change. It's impossible to draw up a road map for the future, but here are some strategic ideas to help give your blog long-term direction:

- **Write an *anchor* post every month or two.** An anchor post is a tutorial-style piece that teaches your readers how to do something, like *How to Pick Fruit at its Peak of Flavor* or *Top 10 Ways to Prevent Rust*. It can be the length of a short magazine article, perhaps 750 to 1,500 words. This type of content is evergreen—it won't become obsolete, and you can continually refer back to it in your subsequent posts. Every month or two, add another anchor post.

- **Write at least one new post a day.** Frequent posting keeps your audience interested and jogs your creativity. The more you post, the more you'll be picked up by the search engines, and the more new people will find your blog and become regular readers. The first two sentences are the hardest of a post, and it's all downhill after that.

- **Comment on other blogs in your niche.** This will attract fellow bloggers and their readers who follow the link in your comment back to your blog. Make a meaningful comment that advances the discussion, don't just say "I agree."

- **Link to other blogs from within your blog posts.** With certain blogging software, this is known as a *trackback*, and leaves a summary of your blog post on the original blog. Result: More bloggers and readers find you.

- **Ask for comments on your blog.** End your posts with a question, prompting your readers for feedback. When practical, end your posts with a question like, "What do you think?", or "What's your take on this?" Readers are often more interested in what *they* have to say than in what *you* have to say.

- **Don't write when you're angry.** If you're upset, cool off for a few hours—or a day—so you don't end up posting something nasty that you might regret later. It's nearly impossible to delete stuff on the Web. You might erase something from your blog, but the text can be archived in dozens of other places.

- **Link to your old content.** After you've been blogging for a while, you'll have five or six previous blog posts that were most popular with readers—drawing lots of links, traffic and comments. For the benefit of new readers, link to these previous posts when you write about the same topics in the future. Add a small menu of these posts on the sidebar of your blog, with a heading such as **Lively Conversations** or **Greatest Hits**.

- **Add artwork.** Sprinkling stock photos and illustrations in your blog posts is a simple way to add visual appeal. Images are eyeball magnets. Writing a post about how to fix a flat tire? Include a small stock photo of someone installing a tire. The site **www.sxc.hu** has thousands of royalty-free photos you can search by keyword. You needn't illustrate your posts literally, which can get boring. Let's imagine your post concerns some type of *manipulation*. It's the key idea and the main word in your post title. How could you illustrate it? Just search for "manipulation" at the photo site mentioned above, and you'll see dozens of images you could use as a smart illustration—like photos of puppets, marionettes or chess pawns. If your first keyword doesn't find results, try a synonym—or if you're feeling ironic, try an antonym.

- **Create an RSS or Atom feed.** Be sure your blog automatically posts a feed, so readers who use an aggregator like Bloglines can read this way if they wish. You may have to turn this function on yourself, so consult your blogging service's help files.

- **Optimize your blog.** Make sure your blog "pings" the blog aggregators such as Technorati and Bloglines each time you've posted to your blog. That way your new content will be indexed immediately.

An easy way to automate this is to open a free account at **www.Feedburner.com** and enable its free Pingshot feature.

Get more tools

Most bloggers don't have special blogging software installed on their PC, but work on their blog from within a Web browser. Here are the most popular blogging services:

- eBay provides a free hosting platform and built-in exposure to shoppers. Go to **http://blogs.ebay.com**

- **Blogger.com.** Owned by Google since 2003. It's free and easy. There's an add-on program enabling you to post to your blog from Microsoft Word. You can use Blogger's free Web space, Blogspot.com, but it's best to keep your content on a domain you control, like Your-Name.com. Do this by using Blogger's FTP feature. For instructions:

- **Help.Blogger.com/bin/topic.py?topic=8917.** Other blogging systems have similar options: You can publish free on their Web space, or publish on your own domain.

- **TypePad.com.** TypePad is a flexible and professional-looking platform, but takes a bit longer to learn than Blogger. Still, you'll have many options for personalizing your blog without having to learn HTML computer code. Basic service costs $4.95 a month; the Plus level costs $8.95 a month and gives you up to three blogs hosted on your own domain. A 30-day free trial is available.

- **WordPress.com.** Set up a free blog, or upgrade to a fuller-featured service. All that's required to begin is a user name and e-mail address.

Blog-to-e-mail service

Loyal readership is key to your blog's success, so make it easy for first-time visitors to keep reading. One of the simplest ways for readers to receive your blog posts is by e-mail subscription.

FeedBlitz.com and Feedburner.com operate two popular, free blog-to-e-mail services. Both provide a snippet of code you can insert on your blog to display a sign-up box or button where readers can provide their e-mail address. Subscribers receive an e-mail digest of any new blog posts, and can click through to your site to read more.

A subscription service makes it more likely that readers will stay with you because they won't need to remember to return to your Web site. An e-mail service is a simple solution for your customers who might not understand how to use Bloglines or other newsreaders.

Only about 20 percent of blog readers understand newsreaders, "so if you're not using e-mail, you're missing 80 percent of your potential audience," says Phil Hollows, chief executive of FeedBlitz.

FeedBlitz's free service also includes some reporting tools showing how many of your e-mails are opened and which of your post headlines readers click most. Knowing which of your posts gets the biggest response is a valuable insight, showing you what content readers value most.

Some businesses that previously published monthly e-mail newsletters have abandoned their newsletters and now deliver similar content in smaller, more frequent chunks using blog-to-e-mail.

E-mail service also provides you with a valuable business asset. You'll have access to those readers directly, so you can send special messages for events like new product releases. This is why many bloggers encourage readers to sign up for e-mail delivery: It provides an automatic marketing channel for special messages about you and your products and services, without having to manually collect contact information by some other means.

The blog-to-e-mail services provide a fully automated double opt-in process, so there's no danger of your blog posts or occasional promotional messages being mistaken for spam.

Blogging systems such as Google's Blogger make it simple for you to post a Profile page, where you can enter a photograph, short biography, and additional contact information. If you think your photo will be helpful, include it on your blog. Your readers will feel a firmer connection if they can see your photo.

Tour blogs

So far, we've explored techniques for luring customers to your blog or Web site. Now we'll turn to blog outreach campaigns—going where part of your potential customer base already congregates.

You can expose your business or products to many more prospects with a series of appearances on blogs catering to your audience—a *blog tour*. Sometimes it's called *guest blogging*.

Blog tours are especially valuable for business owners unable to travel, uncomfortable with public speaking, or whose dispersed customer base makes this impractical. Blog tours can expose your business to a much larger pool of prospects than by attending conferences and trade shows, while requiring less time and money. Blog tours are especially helpful in launching new products and services.

Blog tours are also a good deal for the host blogger, who gets free content for his or her readers.

Typical blog tours include these elements:

- A **guest column** displayed on the host blog to publicize the tour appearance.

- A one-day **appearance**, beginning with an opening statement, a short essay. Then the floor is open for discussion.

- **Follow-up visits** for the next four to seven days to answer questions and comments from blog readers.

Target host blogs

Your first step in arranging a blog tour is finding potential host blogs. Find the most popular blogs read by your target market. Some likely candidates may spring to mind, but new blogs can gain readership quickly, so it's worth surveying the field periodically.

Building your list of target blogs requires some legwork because there is no current, comprehensive directory of all blogs. To determine the popularity, authority and quality of blogs in your niche, you'll need to sample the content yourself.

Start your search here:

- **www.Technorati.com.** This site lists the top 100 most popular blogs at **Technorati.com/pop/blogs**. But to find niche content, you'll need to look beyond these mainstream blogs. Consult the advanced search tool, **Technorati.com/search**, where you can drill down into specific topics.

- **www.Blogsearch.Google.com.** Type in keywords related to your business. Ignore results from personal blogs that focus on the blog author and get little traffic.

- **www.Forbes.com/bow/b2c/main.jhtml.** Forbes' "Best of the Web" directory reviews blogs with high-quality content.

Once you've identified a list of potential blog hosts, prioritize them by three criteria: activity level, reader involvement and traffic volume.

- **Activity level.** How frequently do new posts appear on the blog? Bloggers usually must post new content a few times a week to sustain a loyal readership. Scan the past few months of blog archives to determine the posting frequency.

- **Reader involvement.** How often do readers chime in with thoughtful comments? The vast majority of blogs allow readers to follow up with their own commentary. The frequency and thoughtfulness of reader comments indicates audience engagement.

- **Traffic volume.** Traffic is the natural result of audience loyalty and involvement, and it's an objective measure of a blog's impact. A handy yardstick for measuring blog traffic is **www.Alexa.com**, which provides estimated traffic reports on many Web sites.

At Alexa.com, click **Traffic Rankings** at the top navigation bar. Enter the address of the blog you want to evaluate and click **Get Traffic Details**. For most blogs, you'll see an Alexa rank from 1 (the most-visited site on the Web) to about 5 million, meaning very low readership. For the top 100,000 sites, Alexa provides detailed traffic estimates. Under the heading **Explore this site**, you'll see these links:

- **Traffic Details** shows the blog's relative reach and number of page views, and whether traffic is trending up or down.

- **Related Links** shows other sites popular with the same audience. Here you can discover more blogs frequented by your target audience.

- **Sites Linking In** shows which sites, ranked by authority, have incoming links to the blog. Follow these links, and you'll find more sites targeting your audience.

Depending on the size and nature of your potential customer base, you may find only a few relevant quality blogs, and that's fine. It's better to focus on a small, well-qualified audience who will respond to your message instead of a general audience where you'll have little impact.

Alexa's reports aren't foolproof; they're drawn from a small sample of Web users who use its browser toolbar. Rankings for high-traffic sites are more statistically accurate than reports for niche sites. In any case, Alexa is a handy, free source of objective information about Web traffic, and is more accurate than anecdotal reports. Bloggers and Webmasters are notorious for overestimating their traffic.

Alexa, which is a subsidiary of Amazon.com, isn't limited to blogs, so you can use it to find all sorts of Web sites targeting your niche. Another source of traffic estimates is **www.MetricsMarket.com**.

Know Google PageRank

Another way of determining how much juice a blog has is Google PageRank. It's a patented method Google uses to rank the importance of Web sites on a scale of 1 to 10 based on the authority of incoming links. Google offers a free toolbar you can use to check rankings:

http://toolbar.google.com

Quality blogs and Web sites will have a PageRank of at least five. To determine PageRank, check the blog's main page or a Web site's home page; other pages often are unranked.

Build your guest column

Now that you've identified where you'd like to appear on your blog tour, the next step is creating your guest column. The guest column is an online document providing a description of you and your business, along with one or more photographs.

Your guest column serves three purposes:

- To persuade the blogger to host your appearance.
- To promote your appearance to the blog's readers.
- To prepare the blog audience to discuss your ideas and products.

Essential information like your name and business name should be embedded and visible on the author photo. That way, if a Webmaster accidentally leaves out part of your text—or it's deleted at some point—readers will still have enough information to find your Web site. If possible, combine all the elements of your guest column into a single document to ensure it's displayed properly and nothing is omitted.

A typical excerpt includes these elements:

- A brief description of your products and services, and your existing customer base.

- Features and pricing of your products and services.

- Testimonials from satisfied customers.

- Links to your Web site or to online retailers where your products are sold.

Sell with guest columns

Imagine you're riding in an elevator with a potential customer. You have 20 seconds before the elevator door opens and your companion leaves. What can you say to compel him or her to walk to the nearest computer and buy your product right away? The answer is the heart of your guest column.

More elements for a compelling guest column:

- **Give chunks, not boulders.** Confine the discussion to *the most essential, engaging* nuggets of information you can provide. One way to build an effective guest column is by compiling a short list of hints, like "Top 10 ways to save money when buying a camera" or "Three ways to take better photos.

- **News angle.** Try to find a news hook to pique interest. Is there a current controversy or movie related to your field? Topicality is blog oxygen. For fiction and nonfiction, a strong current-events hook can persuade A-list bloggers to host your tour.

- **Benefits, not features.** What makes your products unique, and what can they do for the customer better than competitors? If you've received a truly impressive testimonial or endorsement, include it.

- **White space.** Break up your text. Separate paragraphs with blank lines, inserting some white space between the gray blocks of text. Readers are more likely to read your excerpt if they can scan chunks of text.

- **All together now.** If your guest column is accompanied by more than one image, assemble everything in a layout file in PDF or HTML format. This prevents the blogger or Webmaster from losing a piece of your excerpt.

Don't send your excerpt as an e-mail attachment. Most people are apprehensive of receiving files from unfamiliar people. Instead, post the document on a dedicated page on your domain, and provide the link. Then your hosts can copy the document or link to it. After you've posted the file on your domain, don't delete it, because some blogs will link to your page instead of keeping the material on their site. The excerpt on your domain may get traffic for years to come.

Pitch to bloggers

Now your column is ready and you've compiled a list of blogs for your tour. It's time to pitch your tour to the host bloggers. Contact each blogger individually by e-mail, explaining why your appearance would be of interest. Provide two or three compelling reasons why your tour will be thought-provoking and entertaining for *this blog's audience.*

Start with your top prospects and work your way down as time permits. Contact bloggers directly; don't simply leave a comment on their blog and hope they notice it. Most blogs have a mechanism for contacting the blogger through an e-mail address or contact form.

Sometimes the more popular a blogger is, the harder it is to get their attention. If you can't find contact information, look at the bottom of the home page, where you may see instructions for contacting the "Webmaster." Sometimes an "advertise with us" link is the most reliable way of reaching a decision-maker.

Tailor your pitch for each blogger, addressing them by name, otherwise your message can be mistaken for spam. Provide your complete contact information including phone number, which also differentiates your message from spam. The subject line of your e-mail must be specific; a generic "Please read this" often is deleted unread.

The guest column includes everything the blogger needs to decide whether to approve your tour appearance. If approved, a copy of the excerpt can be posted at the host blog to promote your appearance in the days preceding the tour. Schedule no more than three to five blogs per week, which should keep you busy.

Make a pitch

Here's a sample script for pitching your blog tour:

SUBJECT: [YOUR NAME] as guest on [BLOG NAME]

Dear [BLOGGER NAME]

I'm a regular reader of your blog, and believe it's one of the best sites about [TOPIC]. I'm writing to see if you would consider having me as a guest on your blog on Monday, May 9, to discuss [TOPIC].

I believe my [PRODUCTS, SERVICES] are of particular interest to your readership. [REASONS, BRIEFLY]

I'm hoping to have a dialog with your readers. If you approve, I'll take a day on your blog, make an opening statement, and respond to comments as long as they keep coming.

I hope you'll give this a try. I've prepared a guest column in an HTML document, which you can view here at my site: http://www.example.com. You're free to reproduce this document on your site or provide links.

Thanks for your consideration,
[SIGNATURE]
[PHYSICAL ADDRESS]
[PHONE NUMBER]

Not every blogger will accept your pitch, and you shouldn't take the rejections personally—an acceptance rate of 25 percent is a good target. Some sites simply don't use content that isn't written by its staff. Often blogs run by newspapers or magazines don't use third-party content except in sections labeled "opinion" or "to the editor."

As realistically as possible, pitch yourself as a potential long-term partner, not a drive-by opportunist. Successful blog tours will prompt return invitations and can launch a mutually beneficial relationship.

Your guest appearance. On the day of your blog tour appearance, open with a short statement, recapping the themes expressed in your guest column, and ask the blog audience for its reaction. Depending on how the blogger administers the site, you may be given a login and password for the site, or simply e-mail your material to the blogger.

Reaction from the blog audience can continue for several days, giving you the opportunity to reappear, replying to comments and answering questions.

Encore appearances. Blog tours don't always cause a big spike in sales or new clients, but they do contribute to word of mouth. Each time you appear in front of your target audience, it's a plus. When a blog appearance goes particularly well, don't let it end there. Offer to write a monthly guest column for the blog in exchange for a link to your site.

Pay for advertising

Unlike most advertising, with pay-per-click (PPC) you don't pay fees each time your ad is displayed, but only when someone clicks on your ad and is taken to your Web site. PPC has revolutionized online promotion, and has been wonderfully effective for many Internet businesses. The prime advantage of PPC is its ability to deliver your ad to targeted audiences.

Although PPC can bring targeted traffic to your site, it's unlikely you'll convert enough of those visitors into immediate buyers unless you have unique, high-priced products or services. Google, for example, will charge you 75 cents or more per click for competitive keywords, and only a small fraction of those clicks will result in sales.

Use Google AdWords

With AdWords, advertisers write short three-line text ads, then bid on keywords relevant to their ad. The ads appear alongside relevant search results or on content pages. For example, to advertise your tropical fish business, you might bid on several different keywords and phrases—**aquarium**, **exotic fish**, **fishkeeping**, and **pet fish**. Depending on how popular those words and phrases are with other advertisers, you might have to pay a minimum of 10 cents, 30 cents, or several dollars for each click. The higher your bid, the higher your ad shows up on the relevant page.

Learn more about Google's AdWords program at:

www.Google.com/Adwords/Learningcenter

You may, however, profit from PPC advertising if you take a long-term view. Do you know how much your customers are worth? If you get any repeat business at all, your customers are worth more than the profit margin from a single sale. If your average customer buys four items during the lifetime of their relationship with you—and your average net profit on those four items is $14 apiece—your average customer is worth $56.

If each of your customers is worth $56, would you spend a few dollars on advertising to attract more new customers?

The most familiar PPC ads are the ubiquitous Google "Sponsored Links" that appear alongside search results or on content-related websites. But Google is no longer the only game in town. eBay and Amazon.com have recently jumped into the PPC game, which could present new opportunities for all kinds of businesses.

Businesses that use PPC ads target their customers by bidding on keywords related to what they're selling. For example, if you're selling scuba-diving equipment, you might bid on the keywords **snorkeling** or **diving**. If you bid sufficiently high, your ad will appear on relevant Web sites when someone searches for your keyword. You pay for the ad only when someone clicks on it, and the more popular the keyword, the more you'll pay. An obscure keyword might be available for a nickel per click on some networks, while a highly competitive keyword might cost as much as $50 per click.

Until recently, Google AdWords and Yahoo Search Marketing were practically the only alternatives for PPC, with Google commanding a lion's share of the market. But things are changing. Just a few short years ago, PPC was called "search engine advertising" because ads were always displayed alongside search results at Google, Yahoo, or another search engine. Sometimes the only thing differentiating your ad from a natural (or organic) search result was the small label "Sponsored Link."

PPC was viewed as a revolutionary way of advertising because you spent money to attract people who had already expressed an interest in what you were selling. In the past couple of years, Google seems to have perfected PPC with its AdWords program. Not only are ads shown alongside search results, but they also pop up on millions of Web sites—relevant blogs, commerce sites, forums, etc. Like all good things, Google has earned so much money serving up PPC ads that other big Internet players have decided to make a run at it too.

Using adMarketplace, Clickriver

Since advertisers have driven up the bidding on many popular PPC keywords in the past several years, PPC isn't a particularly effective way to sell individual low-priced items. But two new wrinkles have popped up in PPC just recently that are providing new opportunities. First, adMarketplace, which had been selling PPC ads exclusively on eBay, has branched out. The program is now open to all online marketers, not just eBay users, and ads may be directed to a variety of sites, including search engines like Ask.com, LookSmart and other shopping-related Web sites.

Meanwhile, Amazon has introduced its own PPC network, Clickriver, a system that displays ads on its product detail pages and can be used to direct traffic to your own Web site or anywhere else. Amazon's ad network reaches about 60 million registered online buyers. The plain-text ads appear about halfway down product detail pages under the heading "Customers viewing this page may be interested in these Sponsored Links."

First, the good news: Clickriver is much easier to use than Google AdWords. The interface is clean and it responds fast. If you ask for a keyword, your ads begin appearing within seconds. It's also relatively cheap compared with Google because many keywords cost just 10 cents per click. Perhaps the low prices indicate that not many advertisers are competing for the keywords, at least not yet.

Clickriver does a great job of suggesting additional keywords. For example, let's imagine you sell orchid growing supplies. Once Clickriver knows you're targeting orchids, it will suggest every book title and author name in the orchid space, at least those with good sales records. This helps you get your ad in front of the right people. It sounds obvious, but you'd be surprised how many good keywords Clickriver will suggest that you didn't think of.

Keywords aren't the only prospecting tool on Clickriver. You can also target entire categories in Amazon's bookstore in one fell swoop. For example, if you wanted your ad to appear on all Amazon book pages related to "gardening," you'd create a new ad and use the keywords "category gardening."

And now, the bad news: Clicks are very, very sparse with Clickriver. It's very likely that the low click-through rate is because Clickriver ads just aren't that visible on Amazon's detail pages. Visibility will probably always be a tension for this program: For Amazon to make serious money with this, they're going to have to raise the profile of the ads. But the more the ads dominate the page, the more buyers will be distracted from buying the Amazon product they were shopping for in the first place.

See the future of PPC

Like many other Internet tools, PPC is evolving at a breakneck pace. So far in this section, we've examined only "keyword-based" PPC systems. But there's a whole other world of PPC that can work for online marketers, known as "product PPC" or "price comparison PPC." Some well-known examples of these are Shopzilla.com, NexTag.com, BizRate.com, Shopping.com, and PriceGrabber.com. It works like this: Participating advertisers upload a list of their inventory. When visitors search for a product, the links to various advertisers show up. Advertisers who pay more are given prominence, but users can also sort the listings to find the lowest price. Each time a visitor buys, the advertiser pays a fee.

It's likely that the competition for PPC advertisers will heat up significantly in the future. Microsoft is also getting into the act, too, with a PPC network called MSN adCenter.

Recommended reading

Three Weeks to eBay Profits: Go from Beginner to Successful Seller in Less than a Month by Skip McGrath, 2006.

eBay Income: How Anyone of Any Age, Location, and/or Background Can Build a Highly Profitable Online Business with eBay by Cheryl L. Russell, 2006.

The Home-Based Bookstore: Start Your Own Business Selling Used Books on Amazon, eBay or Your Own Web site by Steve Weber, 2005.

Titanium eBay:: A Tactical Guide to Becoming a Millionaire PowerSeller by Skip McGrath, 2006.

eBay: Top 100 Simplified Tips & Tricks by Julia Wilkinson, 2006.

Estate Sale Prospecting for Fun and Profit with Craigslist and eBay by John Landahl, 2006.

What to Sell on eBay and Where to Get It by Chris Malta and Lisa Suttora, 2006.

eBay PowerSeller Secrets by Brad and Debra Schepp, 2007.

The eBay Seller's Tax and Legal Answer Book. Cliff Ennico, 2007.

How to Start and Run an eBay Consignment Business by Skip McGrath, 2006.

Word of Mouth Marketing: How Smart Companies Get People Talking by Andy Sernovitz, 2006.

Duct Tape Marketing: The World's Most Practical Small Business Marketing Guide by John Jantsch , 2007

eBay For Dummies by Marsha Collier, 2006.

The Official eBay Bible by Jim Griffith, 2007.

Buzz Marketing with Blogs For Dummies by Susannah Gardner, 2005.

How and Where to Locate the Merchandise to Sell on eBay by Michael P. Lujanac, 2007.

The New Influencers: A Marketer's Guide to the New Social Media by Paul Gillin, 2007.

How to Buy, Sell, and Profit on eBay by Adam Ginsberg, 2005.

More great eBay resources

Selling on eBay is a never-ending, continuous education process. Fortunately, there are many free resources to help you stay abreast of the changing environment and gain new insights to help your business:

Seller Central. This part of eBay's Web site is a central repository for seller tips, services and information, including best practices, most-watched items, and category strategies. See:

http://pages.ebay.com/services/sellerservices.html

Hot items by category. eBay prints a list of the best-selling items on its site each month. Each category is analyzed for bidding and listing activity:

http://pages.ebay.com/sellercentral/whatshot.html

General Announcement Board. This official eBay page includes the most recent eBay news on site changes, promotions, new features, and other news. See:

http://www2.ebay.com/aw/marketing.shtml

eBay Pulse. This section of eBay's Web site displays several lists, updated constantly, showing popular searches, products, items and Stores. You can use this area to determine what buyers are looking for on eBay, across the site and within certain categories. See:

http://pulse.ebay.com/

eBay Radio. eBay's online radio show includes news and helpful tips about managing your eBay business. Listen to the shows on your computer or download to a portable music player. The host is Jim "Griff" Griffith, the dean of eBay University. See:

http://www.ebayradio.info

Community Calendar. Get the latest on eBay events such as Town Halls and workshops, eBay Live and trade shows. See:

http://pages.ebay.com/community/events/index.html

AuctionBytes. Independent reporting on eBay and other online auctioning and selling venues. Valuable resources including news articles, newsletters, videos, and podcasts. See:

http://auctionbytes.com/

eBay University. Live and online classes are held on elementary selling, creating great listings, using advanced tools and marketing your business. See:

http://pages.ebay.com/university/index.html

Answer Center. This member-to-member forum allows eBay members to ask questions and provide information about eBay. See:

http://pages.ebay.com/community/answercenter/

eBay Business. This section of eBay's Web site provides tips, and special offers on products and services that help sellers manage and grow their eBay business. See:

http://pages.ebay.com/businessmarketplace/index.html

There are many other great instructional resources for people starting an eBay business. Many community colleges offer classes on small-business startups, and some of them are focused on eBay in particular. Another place to find help is SCORE, the Service Core of Retired Executives at **www.score.org**. This group of experienced business leaders can offer valuable advice to new entrepreneurs.

eBay jargon cheat sheet

To excel on eBay, it helps to know the lingo. Here's the specialized vocabulary used in the world's top auction Web community:

Administrative Cancellation. A bid's administrative cancellation by eBay in cases such as bidders becoming unregistered.

Account Guard. The eBay Toolbar security feature. It identifies verified eBay or PayPal Web pages and warns of fake or spoof sites. The Account Guard provides a warning when members are about to send an eBay password to a non-eBay site.

Announcement Boards. Web pages containing official eBay news and announcements. They provide information on system status, new features, special promotions, policy changes, and special event information.

Answer Center. A section of eBay's Web site where you can enter questions and get help from other eBay members.

Auction-Style Listing (Online Auction Format). The most commonly used method of eBay selling. Bids are collected for a certain amount of time, and the item sells to the highest bidder.

Best Offer. Listing feature permitting buyers to make an offer to the seller. Can be used with Auction, Fixed Price, and Store listings.

Best Match. When conducting an eBay search, "Best Match" is one of the options in "Sort by." Best Match displays items most relevant to the search, based on shopping of other buyers and other factors.

Bid Assistant. Allows buyers to create a group of items with maximum bids. Bid Assistant bids on items automatically, starting with the item ending first, until an item is won.

Bid Cancellation. When sellers cancel an auction bid in certain situations, such as when the seller is unable to verify the bidder's identity, even after trying to make contact. To prevent a specific user from bidding, sellers can use the Block Bidders/Buyers feature. Canceling bids is discouraged and is restricted by several rules.

Bid Increment. Amount by which a new auction bid must increase from a previous bid to be accepted. Bid increments are based on existing high bids. If the high bid for an item is $6 and the bid increment is 50 cents, the next bid that can count is $6.50.

Bid Retraction. When buyers cancel an auction bid. Retractions are permitted only in special cases, such as when a buyer accidentally enters a bid of $100 instead of $10. Retracting such a bid is allowed if the correct bid is entered immediately.

Bidder. A buyer who bids on an eBay auction.

Bidder Search. Searching for all the items an eBay member has placed bids on for the past 30 days. To enhance privacy, however, some of the items a member has bid on might not be displayed. Also, to enhance security, eBay doesn't display User IDs when the highest bid, fixed price or reserve price reaches a certain value. On bidding detail pages, only the item's seller can view bidders' User IDs.

Blackthorne. An eBay tool that helps sellers create listings in bulk, monitor their listings, and manage customer messages. Blackthorne Pro is designed for high-volume sellers.

Block Bidders/Buyers. Sellers can create this list of eBay members who are prohibited from bidding on or buying your items. Sellers who have a negative experience with a buyer often add them to their Blocked Bidder/Buyer List.

Buy It Now. Instead of auctioning, the seller names a fixed price and permits buyers to purchase the item immediately. You can add the feature to auction, Fixed Price, and Store listings.

Category Listings. eBay is organized into categories such as Antiques, Art, Baby, Books, etc. Shoppers can browse the categories to look for items of interest instead of searching by keyword. Sellers choose the category (or multiple categories) where the item fits and will attract the most attention.

Changed User ID Icon. This small image is assigned to members who have obtained a new User ID in the past 30 days. Members retain the same feedback profile. The Changed User icon puts sellers at a disadvantage during the 30-day period, so name changes should be avoided when possible.

Classified Ads. An eBay listing in which sellers can offer items or services for sale to attract potential customers. Interested parties complete a contact form and send their information to the seller.

Completed Listings Search. Buyers and sellers can search for items that have ended during the past 15 days. By searching for similar items, sellers can view closed listings to see recent prices for items they want to sell.

Detailed Seller Ratings. In addition to an overall feedback rating which can be positive, negative or neutral, buyers can leave detailed ratings on four criteria: accuracy of item description, communication, shipping time, and shipping and handling charges. The ratings, which don't count toward overall feedback scores, range from one to five stars, with five stars being the best.

Discussion Boards. eBay hosts message boards where members can exchange views on a multitude of topics about selling on eBay and other matters. See:

http://pages.ebay.com/community/boards

Dispute Console. This area of eBay helps members manage disputes about transactions. Reached through the My eBay section, the Dispute Console manages the **Unpaid Item** and **Item Not Received** processes.

Dutch (Multiple Item) Auction. Sellers can offer more than one identical item for sale in the same listing. More than one buyer can win, unlike regular auctions. Buyers specify the quantity desired and acceptable price. Winning bids are figured by their total value, bid price multiplied by quantity bidded on.

eBay Express. A section of eBay where sellers offer new, name-brand merchandise at fixed prices. See:

http://www.ebayexpress.com

eBay Stores. Each eBay seller has the option of opening an eBay Store featuring all their listed items. On these Web pages, sellers can use custom displays, self-defined categories and offer special promotions.

eBay Time. The time of day at eBay's head office in California in the Pacific Time Zone.

eBay Toolbar. A tool you can add to your Web browser to guard your account and provide quick access to My eBay, Half.com, eBay Express and eBay Motors. Allows easy searching for eBay items when you're off eBay's site.

eBay Alerts. Track items you are bidding on or watching and learn when you're outbid or an item is ending.

Escrow. Procedure where a third party holds the buyer's payment until merchandise is received and approved. Recommended for purchases over $500. eBay strongly recommends use of Escrow.com.

Feedback. System eBay members use to rate their buyer or seller. Transaction partners can leave positive, neutral or negative ratings and a comment, which are logged on member **Feedback Profiles.** Each member has a profile viewable by other eBayers by clicking on the number in parentheses alongside the User ID.

Feedback Score. Measures reputation of eBay buyers and sellers. From each transaction partner, members receive one positive point, zero (neutral) or negative one point. A high score indicates the member has received a large number of positive ratings.

Feedback Star. A star icon next to member feedback scores that changes color to indicate score ranges. A yellow star indicates a member has less than 50 feedback points.

Final Value Fee. A fee eBay charges the seller depending on the selling price of an item. Final Value Fees aren't charged when an auction doesn't receive bids or the high price was below the seller's Reserve Price.

Fixed Price. Listing format that allows sellers to charge a set price. Buyers can pay immediately without bidding. Sellers must have a feedback score of at least 10 or be ID Verified to list at Fixed Price.

Gift Services. This listing option allows sellers to promote an item that has appeal as a gift. A gift box icon is displayed next to the listing on search and browse lists. Can also indicate the seller offers gift wrapping.

Giving Works is an eBay program to facilitate charity selling to benefit nonprofit organizations. When you list, you can indicate you'll donate between 10 percent and 100 percent (minimum $5) of the final sale price to a certified nonprofit. Listings are emphasized with a Giving Works ribbon and you get a receipt for your tax-deductible donation. You also receive a credit for the Insertion and Final Value Fees according to the percentage of the final sale price you donate.

Groups. A collection of eBay buyers and sellers interested in a common thing. By joining or forming a group, you can participate in discussions, polls, newsletters and calendars pertaining to the group.

Guest Buyer. eBay visitors are allowed to pay for a maximum of two items using a credit card before they're required to register at eBay.

Guides. Sellers or buyers can write a guide to share their knowledge on a category or topic. See:

http://pages.ebay.com/community/chat

ID Verified. An icon indicating a seller's identity was confirmed, offering reassurance to buyers. The process is conducted by a third-party company that cross-checks seller contact information.

Insertion Fee. Sellers pay this non-refundable fee to list an item for sale. The fee amount depends on the type of listing.

My eBay. A Web page where you can manage all your eBay activities, including selling, buying, feedback, and account preferences. A link to My eBay appears at the top of every eBay Web page.

New Listing Icon. Shows an item was listed less than 24 hours ago.

New Member/User Icon. Indicates an eBay member registered within the previous 30 days.

PayPal. A payment transfer company owned by eBay and popular with eBay members. Payments are sent from credit cards or bank accounts without requiring the exchange of account information between buyers and sellers.

PayPal Buyer Protection. Offers buyers up to $2,000 of free coverage when using PayPal for qualified listings. Seller must have a feedback score of at least 50, with 98 percent positive.

Picture Icon. Appearing in browse and search lists, indicates that a listing includes a picture of the item in the description.

PowerSeller. eBay sellers who have at least 98 percent positive feedback and a certain monthly dollar transaction volume.

Pre-Approve Bidders/Buyers. Permits some sellers of high-profile listings to create lists of eBay members allowed to bid on or buy an item. Buyers who don't appear on the list must get approval from the seller before bidding.

Privacy Policy. eBay's personal information protection policy. See:

http://pages.ebay.in/help/policies/privacy-policy.html

Private Auction Listing. Where User IDs aren't displayed to other members. The high bidder and seller are notified via e-mail. Useful for sales of items where bidders might not want to reveal their User ID.

Proxy Bidding. Prevents eBay buyers from having to log in and submit new bids each time they're outbid. eBay automatically bids on the buyer's behalf up to a maximum indicated by the buyer. If the buyer is outbid, eBay raises the bid above other existing bids until the maximum is reached.

Relisting. Listing an item after it fails to sell initially. With some restrictions, eBay automatically refunds the relisting fee when the item sells the second time.

Reserve Price. The lowest price acceptable to the seller in an auction. When sellers list, they may set a secret Reserve Price. If the highest bid doesn't reach the reserve, the seller isn't obligated to sell. This optional feature allows sellers to start their auction at a low price, stimulating bidding, while preventing the item from selling too low.

Reviews. Product evaluations written by eBay buyers and sellers.

Second Chance Offer. Sellers can make offers to losing bidders when the winner fails to pay or the seller has a duplicate item. Second

Chance Offers can be created immediately after the auction and up to 60 days later. If the bidder accepts, seller pays a Final Value Fee but no Insertion Fee.

Security and Resolution Center. Location of eBay where members report problems and obtain information about security. See:

http://pages.ebay.com/securitycenter/

Selling Manager. An eBay tool allowing sellers to manage their listing and sales activities within My eBay. Handles listing tracking and post-sales management such as payments, messages and feedback.

Selling Manager Pro. eBay tool that adds additional features to Selling Manager. Allows the listing of items in bulk, sending feedback and messages in bulk, and reports on profits and losses.

Shill Bidding. Placing bids that artificially raise an item's price. eBay policy prohibits a seller's family members, roommates or friends from bidding on one another's items.

Sniping. Placing a last-second bid on an item.

Starting Price. The price where the seller wants bidding to begin.

TurboLister. Free eBay software that automates the creation of multiple listings. See:

http://pages.ebay.com/turbo_lister/

Unpaid Item Process. Sellers can use this dispute resolution procedure when they don't receive payment for a sold item. If the outcome isn't satisfactory, the seller can file for a Final Value Fee credit.

User Agreement. Terms under which eBay offers service. Buyers and sellers must agree to the terms before participating on eBay. See:

http://pages.ebay.com/help/policies/user-agreement.html

User ID. The unique name used to identify eBay buyers and sellers. You choose your User ID when registering at eBay.

Want It Now. A section of eBay where buyers can provide a description of what they'd like to buy. Sellers can respond if they have an appropriate item.

Alphabet soup answer key

The following abbreviations are commonly used in eBay listings and discussion boards. You'll also find some of these acronyms in auction descriptions and titles, but remember that many new eBayers will be confused by most of this terminology:

B&W: Black and white

BC: Back cover

BIN: Buy It Now

CIP: Customer initiated payment

DOA: Dead on arrival

EST: Eastern Standard Time

EUC: Excellent used condition

FAQ: A list of frequently asked questions with answers.

FB: Feedback

FC: Fine condition

FVF: Final Value Fee

G: Good condition

GBP: Great Britain Pounds

GU: Gently Used. Item that has been used but shows little wear, accompanied by explanation of wear.

HP: Home page

HTF: Hard to find

HTML: HyperText Markup Language. The language used to create Web pages.

IE: Internet Explorer

IM: Instant messaging

INIT: Initials

ISP: Internet Service Provider - a company that gives you access to the Internet

JPG: Preferred file format for pictures on eBay (pronounced "Jay-Peg")

LTBX: Letterbox. Video format that recreates a widescreen image.

LTD: Limited edition

MNT: Mint. In perfect condition (a subjective term)

MIB: Mint in box

MIJ: Made in Japan

MIMB: Mint in mint box

MIMP: Mint in mint package

MIP: Mint in package

MNB: Mint no box

MOC: Mint on card

MOMC: Mint on mint card

MONMC: Mint on near-mint card

MWBT: Mint with both tags

MWMT: Mint with mint tags

NARU: Not a registered user (or suspended user)

NBW: Never been worn

NC: No cover

NIB: New in box

NM: Near mint

NOS: New old stock

NR: No reserve price for an auction-style listing

NRFB: Never removed from box

NWT: New with tags

NWOT: New without original tags

OEM: Original equipment manufacturer

OOP: Out of print

PL: A Pink or a Pinkliner. This refers to an eBay staff member who posts a message on a Discussion Board. Messages from eBay staff have a pink header.

PM: Priority Mail

PST: Pacific Standard Time

RET: Retired

SCR: Scratch

S/O: Sold out

Sig: Signature

SMS: Short Message Service. Text messaging for a wireless device, such as a mobile phone.

SYI: Sell Your Item form

TM: Trademark

UPI: Unpaid Item

URL: Uniform Resource Locator. The address that identifies a Web site (such as www.ebay.com).

USPS: United States Postal Service

VF: Very fine condition

VHTF: Very hard to find

WS: Widescreen (same as letterbox)

XL: Extra large

A final word

eBay is a special universe that offers bold opportunities to anyone willing to put in the effort. The following letter, posted on eBay's Web site in 1996 by the company's founder, Pierre Omidyar, captures eBay's guiding principles:

I launched eBay on Labor Day, 1995. Since then, this site has become more popular than I ever expected, and I began to realize that this was indeed a grand experiment in Internet commerce.

By creating an open market that encourages honest dealings, I hope to make it easier to conduct business with strangers over the Internet.

Most people are honest. And they mean well. Some people go out of their way to make things right. I've heard great stories about the honesty of people here. Occasionally you may meet people who are not honest. It's a fact of life.

Here, those people can't hide. We'll drive them away. Protect others from them. And this depends on your active participation. Become a registered member. Use eBay's Feedback

Forum. Give praise where it's due — make complaints where appropriate. Let everyone know what a joy it was to deal with someone.

Above all, conduct yourself in a professional manner. Deal with others the way you would have them deal with you. And remember: at eBay, you're usually dealing with individuals, just like yourself. People sometimes make mistakes. That's just human. We can live with that. We can deal with that. We can still make deals with that.

Thanks for participating. Good luck and good business!

Regards,
Pierre

Index